Egon Karl Walz

Monetary democracy and climate policy in consideration of efficiency

Egon Karl Walz

Monetary democracy and climate policy

in consideration of efficiency

Rediroma-Verlag

Bibliografische Information der Deutschen Nationalbibliothek:
Die Deutsche Nationalbibliothek verzeichnet diese Publikation in der Deutschen Nationalbibliografie; detaillierte bibliografische Daten sind im Internet über http://portal.dnb.de abrufbar.

ISBN 978-3-96103-568-7

www.rediroma-verlag.de
9,95 Euro (D)

Foreword to the English edition

Dear Reader,

In the German language, the title 'Denkanstoss' means that one gets a 'food for thought' to make one start to think. And this is exactly my goal.

As a German author, the examples and arguments are from my environment. The topicality of the examples is December 2018. However, similar structures can be found in every country. Monetary democracy can be introduced in any form of government. It makes democratic constitutions more democratic. For the European Union in particular, monetary democracy offers an opportunity to create a confederation of states close to the citizens. Monetary climate policy is a complementary approach to an expanded international climate agreement. This booklet therefore contains impulses for new political actions for everyone.

I would like to thank all the people who supported me in the production and translation of this book.

Index of contents

1. Composition and structure of the book

Albert Einstein was awarded his Nobel Prize for the photoelectric effect, which today is based on the solar cells. The award was not for the already experimentally confirmed theory of relativity[a]. One of the forward-looking statements of the theory of relativity is that the time is not absolute, it runs everywhere and not equal in space. To dispose this familiar obviousness, was too bold. With the GPS navigation devices, so that we know today, is taken into account that the clocks in the satellites run differently than here on the Earth's surface[b].

Also the concept of monetary democracy disposes much-loved obviousness, see Chapter 8. The concept can be derived successively from mathematical axioms. It is based in different areas of knowledge and can be considered 'sui generis'[c].

Therefore the following structure of the book is selected allowing a selected checkup of the complex subject. In Chapter 2 'Basic concept of monetary democracy' the concept is consistently presenting specific possible economic examples. While I refer to Chapter 3, in which specific assumptions are explained and other possible approaches are discussed.

Who gets the feeling in this presentation that the introduction of monetary democracy must fail on the complex intergovernmental interrelations and related decision-making processes, please jump to Chapter 6 (implementation of monetary democracy), before putting the book away.

[a] For details see e.g. Wikipedia

[b] Twin paradox

[c] Unique in its characteristics

The concept can gradually and steadily be implemented since (almost) all items exist in details that are already proven.

They, who feel that the theory is too 'dry' or don't like the details, can jump directly to Chapter 5 where the fantastic monetary possibilities are shown in democracy exemplary examples.

In Chapter 7 (climate) you will find a version adapted to this book, which was written 3 years ago and published 2 years ago in the network, called "Monetary climate policy in consideration of efficiency". In Chapter 7.1 "Thesis on climate policy", I argue that the previous steps and existing structures for an effective, world-wide environmental and climate policy must be supplemented adequately and necessarily.

This book is aimed to politically responsible and interested parties, as well as to the general population. In Chapter 4 (basic recognition), everybody can check whether his world view corresponds with my opinion.

The book is also intended for scientists in various fields: by economists, political scientists up to sociologists. I urge them to contradict me or correct me. I am thankful for a discourse that could lead to a more experienced version of this book.

Monetary democracy has no answer to the global challenge of the exponentially growing population. I see only marginal influences on the Damocles sword of turbo capitalism.

The monetary democracy, however, is an evolutionarily supplement to be introduced and provides an additional approach for climate and environmental protection, for the preservation and expansion of sustainable infrastructure and stabilise democratic systems directly. In this sense I quote Simon Peres: The future is not a continuation of the past.

2. Basic concept of monetary democracy

2.1 Overview and objectives

Monetary democracy is a complement to state and supranational (especially European) constitutions. The citizen is given the opportunity to exert direct influence on part of the public budget, with every vote counting equally.

In this concept, money will also be generated, with the focus on self-interest and the common good, and the principle of profit maximisation is abandoned.

Self-interest is met by a funded pension. The citizen promotes the projects which he sees as most urgent and important in the area of climate and environmental protection as well as infrastructure.

Obstacles arising from various public responsibilities will be overcome. Subsidy and promotion policy can be newly regulated and controlled. Projects in the fields of environment and infrastructure can also be initiated and supported by minorities. The 'royal right' of the parliaments to decide on the budget is not curtailed, but the parliaments are relieved.

Monetary democracy has further positive effects:

- Identification of people within Europe and their homeland
- Reduction of the influence of turbo-capitalism
- Effective use of funds and reduction of corruption

- Elimination of competition for public-private partnerships (PPP)
- Addressing the pension issue over the long term
- Relief of public budgets

This brief overview illustrates the scope and complexity of monetary democracy. However, this does not prevent a gradual introduction as proposed in Chapter 6.

With the model of monetary democracy, we expect to give a THOUGHT-PROVOKING (DENKANSTOSS) impulse and in this sense quote Prof. Dr. Harald Heinrichs, sustainability researcher and sociologist, Leuphana University Lüneburg[1]: "Sustainable action and decision making starts with the individual, but the individual alone will not really be able to advance sustainability in the world. This only works if people change overall. This only works if the framework conditions change and if it is made easy for people to realize their basic inclination to act sustainably."

2.2 Cash flow in the monetary democracy

The focus is on a publicly guaranteed, inflation-protected pension fund (see 3.1). This pension fund has 3 inflows:

- from the government
- from private persons
- and from realized projects (see 2.3)

The amount of the share of the public budget that the citizens themselves can define is determined by a basic monthly contribution from the government. For each participant (see 3.2 - hereinafter also referred to as private individuals), the government (see 3.3) transfers a monthly basic contribution of - assumed here - € 10 (see 3.4) to the pension fund.

Private individuals can invest to a limited extent in the pension fund through a savings plan or a one-off payment (see 3.5), thereby increasing their pension entitlements (see 3.6).

A monthly comparison between cash inflows and outflows and citizens' votes, decides which projects are financed and released (see 2.6).

2.3 Project types

2.3.1 Project types according to cash flow

- Project with regular reflux ('money printing machines')

  Example: Wind turbines, toll roads, grids

  The laws of capitalism stipulate that investments must be profitable, i.e. profit maximization or a good interest-bearing investment. The electricity grids in Germany serve as an example. The capital investors receive a sufficient profit, which is raised by the net remuneration payments of the consumers. Here in monetary democracy we give up the principle of profit maximization and can therefore realize projects which we regard as basic supplies by the government. This is an argument that can be omitted by public private partnerships.

- Projects with interest-bearing repayments ('projects on credit')

  Example: Energetic renovation of houses

  The energetic renovation is completely financed by monetary democracy. The owner of a house has no additional financial burden. The repayment of the investment sum is interest-bearing through the saving of the related energy over the years. If the savings have balanced the received investment needs, then the house owner will profit afterwards from the lower energy costs. Thus promotion programs of the state become void, a house owner escapes a credit risk and a substantial step for reaching the climatic goals can be converted immediately.

- Financial projects (so-called 'assets')

  Example: Purchase of shares in sustainably operating companies and existing companies in the energy sector, e.g. electricity grids, wind farms, etc.

  Such plants have several advantages and effects.

  Sustainable and socially responsible companies usually have higher costs than profit-oriented companies. The capital inflow enables such companies to expand and offer their positively designed products to the market even at lower returns. They are therefore protected from ruinous competition from companies with strong capital resources.

  Acquisitions of shares in companies such as electricity grids, solar power plants, etc. stabilize these companies. On the other hand, these companies achieve a real profit that can be predicted over decades. Thus the contributions paid by the 'little man' through the EEG levy are automatically transferred into his own pension entitlements.

- Projects without capital return ('project support')

  Example: Bridge renovation, rough or detailed planning of a project, sewage treatment plant in India. These types of projects serve to maintain and repair infrastructures and part of the development aid that the citizens want in terms of climate or environmental policy.

2.3.2 Single projects and programs

A further criterion for distinguishing between project types is a single project or a project that runs as part of a program. This distinction is important for clearance and approval. This includes, for example, programs for house insulation, solar cells, solar ovens.

2.3.3 Specific national projects

So far, environment, climate and infrastructure have been mentioned as project topics. Responsible parliaments can finance other project topics through the pension fund. This is essentially dependent on the existing support measures within a government. An example of this in Germany is funding with IUDC (Integrated Urban Development Concept), starting with complete financing of monitoring and evaluation through to implementation of a funding measure.

2.3.4 Projects of foreign aid

German development aid policy has changed over the last decades depending on the government coalition. Today, the aim is to encourage companies to invest in African countries. The aim is to create jobs. Individual energy projects, such as wind turbines and solar power plants, could also be financed by the pension fund after planning and responsibility of the country of origin. Changes in the law in the country may also become necessary in order to fulfil the criteria of a project application. This was the case, for example, in Nigeria[2]. Since transparency is required, the corruption lamented by German Development Aid can be minimised.

Infrastructure measures can also be promoted through the coordination of the participants in other countries. The decision as to who will receive funding depends very much on the reports of the journalists. Countries that do not uphold democratic values or violate human rights are unlikely to receive any financial aid from the European population. In the absence of votes this can be understood as 'punishment', as described by experimental economic research[3].

2.3.5 Ownership and possession conditions

There are no restrictions here. Roads, public transport are owned by public authorities. Wind farms can be owned by joint stock companies, cooperatives or private individuals. Energetic house renovations are possible with different owners. Important for monetary democracy are the names of the persons responsible for the project and the responsibilities for the maintenance and servicing of the project.

If a project is part-financed and the applicant has to withdraw the application for various reasons or the project is stopped by parliament for political reasons, the funds that have already flowed into this project flow into the project with financial character. This supports the sustainable economy.

Taking efficiency into account, in anticipation of the proposed climate policy, (Chapter 7), it makes sense to label the projects as climate projects, environmental protection projects and infrastructure projects with possible further subdivisions (roads, alternative mobility, digitisation, etc.) for the purposes of statistics and data collection.

2.4 Infrastructure of monetary democracy

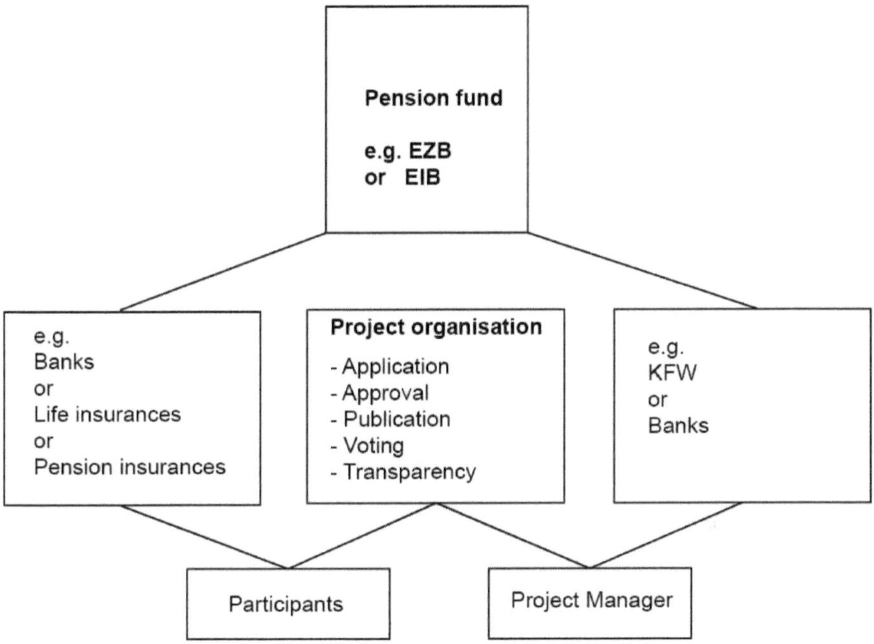

For the implementation of monetary democracy, I see 4 major players for the flow of money and information. The European Investment Bank (EIB) can hold the pension fund's money for Europe. It already managed the Structural and Investment Fund (ESIF) and other funds under the Juncker Plan 2015.

On the right side of the diagram, the project page, I see institutions that have experience in the lending business. These are, for example, the European Investment Bank EIB, the 'Kreditanstalt für Wiederaufbau KFW (Reconstruction Loan Corporation), Federal state banks, or commercial banks. After their release from the pension fund, they receive the corresponding capital to carry out the concrete implementation with the project managers.

On the left side of the diagram, the citizens, I see institutions that have direct contact with the participants. These institutions store personal data about the capital. This is used for additional payments by private individuals, the calculation of pension entitlements and their settlement with the pension fund.

In the centre is a computing centre for the projects. This is where project applications are stored, approved and published, where citizens vote and where transparency for the projects is guaranteed. This data centre could be installed at the project management authority.

This would give citizens two points of contact:

- The citizen's bank account or life insurance, if any, for payments and annuities, as well as information on their invested capital.
- He has access to the computing centre for projects. There he can view the approved projects, carry out his coordination and maintain the transparency of the projects.

A project manager also has only two focal points: the project management authority and his bank, which he uses to handle the financial side of things. Of course, personal data must be cross-checked between data centres and data protection must be ensured.

2.5 From project application to publication

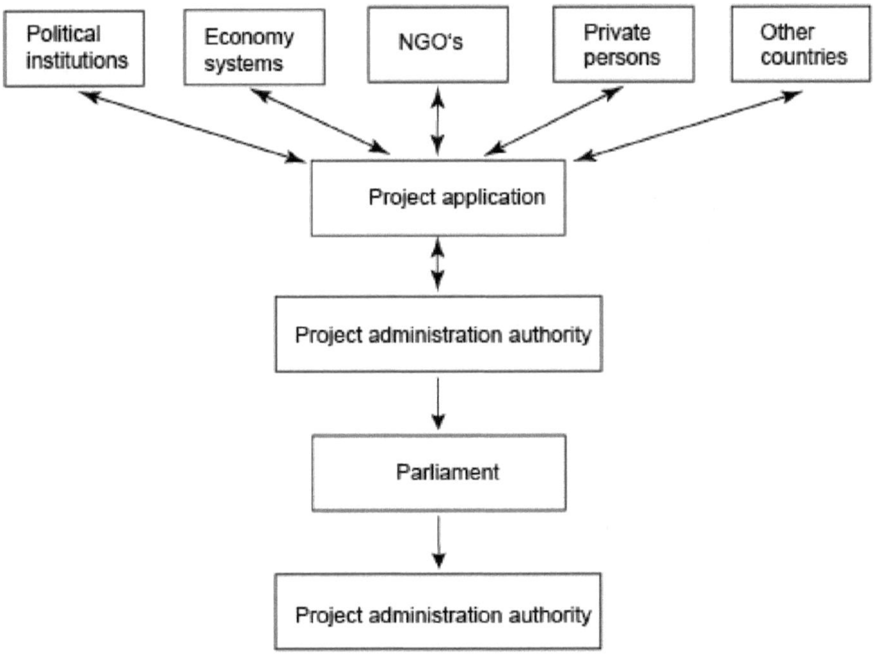

Project applications can be submitted from different areas. These include political institutions, parliaments, local councils, economy systems, NGOs (not governmental organisations), private individuals or other countries. Project applications must meet certain criteria, namely the objectives of monetary democracy, i.e. climate and environmental protection as well as infrastructure measures. In addition, applications must be prepared in such a way that they can be put to the vote. In the case of major projects, this includes detailed planning in order to prevent gross mistakes such as those that occurred at Berlin BER Airport[4].

There are plenty of proposals for structuring these projects in the private sector and in government support programmes. I refer, for example, to the publication of the Federal Ministry for the Environment, Nature Conservation and Nuclear Safety as a working aid for municipalities for the IUDC (Integrated Urban Development Concept) project. In chapter 3.6 you will find how costs and financing overviews or how planning can be presented. The section 'Success factors' contains a basic principle of monetary democracy: 'Successes should be communicated visibly and at an early stage'. Chapter 4.1 states that the implementation of a programme under IUDC places high demands on the responsible players in terms of personnel. In the case of monetary democracy, it should also be mentioned that legal security is required. In the case of countries with which the European Union has not concluded any viable trade agreements, this means in particular that information is provided on the flow of funds and that responsible institutions (NGOs, UNO ...) and project leaders are named.

Contrary to financing in Germany and Europe, in monetary democracy the projects are fully financed. In Germany, the Federal Government grants financial assistance to the federal states in accordance with § 104 b of the Basic Law, which is supplemented by funds from the federal states and local authorities. The introduction of monetary democracy therefore eliminates high bureaucratic and administrative costs as well as a 'competence wrangling'. In the case of subvension, this avoids projects that do not bring any benefits, see chapter 4.10.

Project applications are submitted to the project administration authority. This could involve the EIB or KfW. If the project application is complete and the project application is approved, it goes to the responsible parliament, for me the European Parliament.

Parliament has the option of rejecting individual projects. This can be done for political and ethical reasons. The general approval is already fulfilled by the fact that the authority responsible for managing the projects has forwarded the project applications to Parliament after the preliminary examination. If the projects have been approved by Parliament, they are returned to the project administration authority, which carries out the further bureaucratic processing until they are published on the Internet.

2.6 Coordination and financing of projects

The core of monetary democracy is citizen participation through elections and votes. The amount of freely available capital to be distributed is calculated monthly (see Chapter 3.10) as well as the remaining capital requirement for each project (see Chapter 3.9).

Every private individual is entitled to vote if his or her country pays the basic amount in accordance with Chapter 3.4. Each private individual has 3 votes, whereby accumulation is possible. This allows people to set different priorities and follow the progress of the selected projects more closely.

Like a political election that takes place every 4 to 5 years, there are different voting behaviors. There are voters who regularly go to the polls and feel that this is a civic duty. They are also not eager to be obliged to vote regularly, see also chapter 4.17 'Overtaxing people in our time'. Then there are committed citizens who regularly want to see how projects develop and vote accordingly. This different voting behaviour is taken into account in monetary democracy.

Every month a citizen can assign his vote to another project, if desired. Otherwise, there are projects that the citizen absolutely wants to realise and whose financing must be secured. For this purpose, one or all three votes have to be mandatory assigned to a project. This means that he cannot change his vote until the project has been fully financed. It is then possible for the person responsible for the project to start the project earlier, since the financing is secured by government contributions (see example in chapter 5.1).

A participant therefore has the following options with his votes:

- He can support several projects of different nature, because he has freedom of choice.
- He can assign his voice for a longer period of time to a project which, for example, represents a programme or takes a longer time for realisation.
- He can assign his money grant to a project in a mandatory way. In this way, he helps the project managers to plan their finances in a timely manner.

The votes of non-voters or the votes of voters who cast less than 3 votes are not taken into account in this allocation. They are distributed by the state that paid the basic contribution (see 3.9).

In addition, each participant may contribute capital to the pension fund. The following options are available:

- The capital can be allocated directly to one or more projects. This reduces the capital required for a project.
- The participant does not want to decide on a project. Then the vote can be marked as 'not assigned'. The money then flows into the capital to be distributed to finance the projects. This increases the monthly value of the votes.
- The possibility is supplemented by the project with financial character (investments). This project is managed by a fund manager who strengthens the sustainable economy through ethical criteria (see Chapter 3.1, first paragraph).

The value of a vote is recalculated every month. For this purpose, the freely available capital is divided by the number of valid votes. Then each project is assigned the value of all votes cast for the project. If the sum of all votes assigned to a project reaches the capital requirement, then the project is financed and can be released, see examples under chapters 3.9 and 3.10 as well as the exemplary example under 5.1.

It also makes sense to set a time limit for projects. Projects which, for example, do not receive a vote for two years are not supported by the population and should be cancelled. A new application for such projects is of course possible. Capital that has already been allocated is then to be assigned to the project with financial character.

Given the large number of projects, it is easy for participants to search for projects. It makes sense to structure projects according to type and objectives, such as environmental protection, infrastructure, development aid, etc. At the same time, filters can be added according to various criteria, such as state, degree of financing, type of project, etc. Algorithms such as those used in online department stores are also conceivable, e.g. frequency of topic selection or artificial intelligence that can submit and justify proposals. A standardized and transparent project description is important for the handling.

This procedure of coordination and financing of the projects opens up various possibilities for smaller affected groups, i.e. minorities, to make the world more concrete. This is presented using examples in Chapter 5.

2.7 Project realization and transparency

A project is financed if

- funds were allocated according to the capital requirement for the project,
- binding assignments to a project, be it from the government or from private individuals. According to financial planning, partial orders with advance payments can be awarded earlier.

For each project there is / are one or more persons who are responsible for transparency. This means that, depending on the size of a project, regular or occasional feedback must be entered into the project database. The completion of a project will be published. A post-calculation, as it is already done today to the credit institutes, will be attached. This is an effective means against corruption. In the case of project types with capital reflux, at least annual information must be published after completion.

The transparency of a project can be supported by the published project description:

- FAQs
- Possibility of question/answer
- A link to share with negative experiences of project voters.

This last point is useful in case of controversial technology or known misdemeanors from the project managers. This is a punishment in the sense of experimental economic theory.

For the transparency and control of the projects previous institutions are involved, like the responsible body of the European Parliament or the (to be installed) European Public Prosecutor's Office against subsidy fraud[5]. In addition, there are many participants, who represent a huge potential from a wide variety of disciplines. The investigative press is also called upon to uncover undesirable developments.

If there are obvious differences between the project application and the project implementation, those responsible for the project can be asked to comment. If there is no satisfactory answer, a legal department can be called in. This is where a decision is made on a further procedure. The costs of the legal department are carried out by the entire pension fund. Thus also smaller projects receive a legal protection, even if the costs do not seem to justify this. Each project can develop larger difficulties, which exceeds the framework of the requested investment sum substantially. In this case, a supplementary budget must be approved. The responsible parliament has the possibility here to demand a general stop of the project or to present a positive decision justified to the public. A building stop of the project can be prevented by direct guarantee assumption of the government. Immediate financing can be achieved by the government directly allocating the basic contributions of the non-voters to this project in the following month.

A further transparency concerns the technical implementation. In the case of house insulation projects, financing is provided by saving primary energy. As with a scientific project, standards can be developed here that concern the quantification and measurement of such energy savings. Further technical knowledge can be exchanged and be used for other topics. These include experience with concrete and carbon, bio-wastewater treatment plants and sewerage in developing countries, solar power plants, etc. An internet platform would be an effective support.

Transparency is an essential prerequisite for deciding which project will be chosen by the participants. Prof. Dr. Mausfeld quotes the investigations of two renowned political scientists as follows[6]: "The public opinion and the behaviour of the voters are, in relation to the information provided to them, understandable, justifiable and thus rational in this sense. ... provided that all relevant information is available, the public as a collective has the ability to govern. ... The core of democracy is that information must be available and citizens must be able to debate these things."

This realisation is a challenge to the press, to investigative journalism, to critically accompany the individual projects. The demand also goes to the technicians to be able to announce positive and negative consequences of a technical solution to the population. For this reason, it must be provided that the possibility of making a comment and implementing, in terms of the EDP system on the Internet. Experience must show to what extent a 'clearing house' is to be introduced that brings together conflicting comments or that the clearing house prevents a shitstorm.

3. Statement and discourse to assumptions

3.1 Pension fond

Government pension funds already exist in many different countries. Europe's largest pension fund, which is also the fifth largest pension fund in the world, manages USD 419 billion and is owned by the Netherlands[a7]. It invests in all asset classes of bonds, equities, real estate and hedge funds. The Pension Fund of the USA[b] is the largest pension fund with USD 2,789 billion. Sovereign wealth funds also serve to protect people in old age. The largest belongs to Norway and is worth USD 825 billion[c]. With the establishment of sovereign wealth funds, strategic political action is possible in addition to providing for and safeguarding the population. For example, domestic (or European) companies can be protected against a forced takeover by a foreign investor through a political decision.

In the meantime, funds have also drawn up lists of criteria under public pressure that favour companies that operate according to ethical and sustainable principles. There are active and passive characterisations of sustainability funds. Norges Invest is the pioneer here.

The pension fund of monetary democracy is to earn only a low rate of interest, e.g. 0.5%, but with inflation protection. In Germany, in contrast to France, demand for inflation-hedged government bonds is low. Never-

[a] Stichting Pensioenfonds ABP

[b] Social Security Trust Fund

[c] Norges Invest

theless, the mechanism of low interest rates and inflation protection is known and introduced. The interest paid is calculated on the basis of the inflation-related value of current deposits, i.e. on a monthly basis.

3.2 Participants

By this we mean a natural person who is clearly identified by a tax number and / or a social security number of the pension in their country and has reached the age of 16. This should be all eligible voters in political elections, plus young people over the age of 16.

Young people should be able to participate actively in monetary democracy, as described in Chapter 4.14. In purely legal terms, €10 per month is pocket money, which the young people can determine with their own responsibility.

Private individuals who are already entitled to a pension or receive a pension must also be included. This is because the 10 € is linked to the right to co-determine the expenditure of the government´s budget. It is not an accumulation of assets, but the pension is increased by this amount.

3.3 Nations

All persons who have citizenship or regional voting rights and are registered in the national statutory social security system belong to a government.

The transfer of the contribution for each citizen to the pension fund is a burden on the national budget. On the other hand, it is used to finance projects that are normally included in the budget or to which the government has committed itself internationally (e.g. development aid). Of course, coordination between the projects to be financed in the pension funds and the projects to be retained in the budget is necessary; see also 4.16, Public budgets.

In the federal budget for Germany for 2019[8], 40.4% of the budget of €356.8 billion is earmarked for the Federal Ministry of Labour and Social Affairs, with pensioners and the unemployed receiving most of the money. The amount of 10 € provided here can be considered as part of this resort or as part of the development aid. See the figures in Chapter 3.4. In Germany, the government already transfers money to its citizens with capital-forming benefits or 'Riester' contributions. After the introduction of monetary democracy, these can be omitted or adjusted. Some countries reserve funds for their civil servants in order to be able to meet future pension claims. These could flow into the pension fund in order not to have to be invested in the free capital market with the known negative consequences (see 4.6).

For taxpayers in Germany, the €10 could be seen as a compulsory contribution to a funded pension, as the Swedish pension system does (see 4.11). For the benefit recipients of the social security institutions, it would be a VAT relief for a purchase value of just over €50.

Monetary democracy should and can replace subsidy and subsidy policies in the medium term. This will result in a restructuring of responsibilities between communities, counties, nations, federal government or Europe towards the population. According to the experiences it applies to adapt the public financial planning over the years by a change of the basic contribution of €10.

3.4 Amount of 10 EURO

With the assumed basic contribution of €10 and approx. 70 million participants in Germany, the annual amount is €8.4 billion. This corresponds to approx. 2.35 % of the federal budget for 2019 in Germany. I plead for an introduction throughout Europe and couple the basic contribution to the gross domestic product (GDP), as with development aid. The UN targets of 1970 were 0.7% of GDP[a]. If I take the monthly basic amount of €10 for Germany, the underlying data[b] show only 0.26% of GDP, i.e. less than half the percentage of 0.7% for development aid.

The following summary is given for selected countries:

	Partici-pants in Mio.	GDP Billion USD	Monthly basic amount per particpant in EUR
Bulgaria	6	57	1-2
Germany	70	3685	10,0
France	55	2584	8-10
Greece	9,5	201	3-5
Italy	50	1937	7-8
Netherlands	15	825	10-11
Austria	7,5	417	10-11
Poland	30	525	3-4
Romania	17	211	2-3
Hungary	8	152	3-4

[a] Spiegel online of 11.04.2017
[b] Wikipedia: Participants population minus rough 10 - 15 % for children up to 16 years, GDP with conversion of 0.88 EUR / USD

There are major differences between the countries which are the net recipients of subsidies in Europe. This can be taken into account when introducing modular democracy in Europe (see 6.4). Criticism could arise to the extent that the voices of citizens from poorer countries have less weight than those of economically strong states. This can be justified by the fact that the costs of infrastructure measures in these countries can be realised more cheaply. It could also be agreed that the difference to the highest contribution rates for existing subsidies for these countries would be taken into account. A political decision-making process must be claimed for here.

3.5 Supplement payment from private persons

Today's capital market is characterised by the policy of the European central bank of cheap money.

In 2014, Germany had financial assets in excess of €5,000 billion, of which 39.1% were cash and deposits, 31.1% insurance and old-age provision, 22.1% equity bonds and funds[9]. In the second quarter of 2018, financial assets already amounted to €5,977 billion[a]. In 2015, life insurance policies had a volume of €1,500 billion in Germany and € 1,800 billion in France[b].

The pension fund of monetary democracy is and remains a personal fund for funded pensions. Investors and investment companies are excluded. We therefore take over the proven deposit options for life insurance policies and savings accounts:

- a regular savings plan, whereby suspension periods must be possible
- Single payments from a minimum contribution of 50 €.

[a] ZDF: dpa and German Central Bank

[b] Mittagsmagazin ARD 01.12.2015

In contrast to a Riester subsidy, the contributions paid in are intended exclusively for pension payments. A (complete) repayment, e.g. to finance a residential property, is therefore not possible before the pension is drawn.

The attractiveness of seeing the pension fund as an investment security can be increased by a 'savings book character' of the deposits. This could include:

- Income taxes on interest are not due until disbursements are made.
- Pension payments can already begin at the age of 50 years, in order to make a reduced work time possible in the age or a vocational ‘time out’.
- Annual payments are also conceivable to finance larger purchases. In order to secure the liquidity of the fund and the projects, an annual maximum amount corresponding to the annual pension payments could apply.
- The additional payments represent a personal asset, but with limited access. They are thus also available for credit protection.

The additional payments can be assigned according to personal priority to one project or directly assigned to several projects or made freely available for use. If desired, the name of the depositor can be published with these projects. This serves the reputation of the investor. Prof. Dr. Claus Lamm, Psychologist and Neuroscientist at the University of Vienna[10], explains the motivation of foundations of rich personalities, such as Bill Gates or Ford, for the human necessity of enjoying a reputation as 'good boys'. This need is also exploited by small donations. During the reconstruction of the ‘Frauenkirche’ in Dresden or the ‘Garnisonskirche’ in Potsdam, the names of the donors could/can be embedded in bricks and thus remain visible for future generations.

Furthermore, the additional payments should be upwardly limited. This can be achieved in such a way that the calculated pension entitlement does not exceed an amount of € 3,000 per month as things stand today. This prevents that larger assets can be inherited in an inflation-secured manner or that an abuse can take place through self-interest.

3.6 Entitlement to a retirement pension

The pension entitlement consists of 2 parts. On the one hand, there are the contributions paid to the citizen by the government. The calculation is based on a realistic mortality table in which the capital is incorporated for consumption (with my Riester pension I have to live over 100 years to get my paid-in capital back without interest). The start of the pension should be determined uniformly throughout Europe and should contain components of a 'flexi pension'.

The second part of the pension entitlement is calculated from the additional payments made by private individuals. Here the depositor has the option of using the accumulated amount for consumption, which increases the pension, or as a 'passbook' with inheritance and limited access (see Chapter 3.5).

Life insurers should be able to offer their services for calculating the pension amount, as they are already successfully using the corresponding programs. Of course, a uniform mortality table must be used.

3.7 Death of a private person

In the event of the death of a citizen, the share paid by the State into the pension fund as a contribution lapses. These are taxes paid once, the use of which the citizen could vote on. The capital accumulated here does not represent assets for the citizen, but only an entitlement on an additional pension benefit. For the accumulated capital from the additional payments the country-specific law of the succession tax and the inheritance tax applies. Here every citizen can freely nominate the beneficiary in a will - or leave the money in the fund.

3.8 Administration / legal costs

In addition to capital outflows for new projects and pension payments, funds from the pension fund flow into administration, bureaucracy and data processing, as well as for legal advice. The costs of legal advice are incurred when a project is so difficult that legal action must be taken against the person responsible for the project or a dispute and arbitration procedure must be initiated.

3.9 Capital requirements of a project

The capital requirement of a project, as it was called at the time of application, can be reduced by three factors.

In the case of subsidies in the European Community, it is currently the case that the subsidised country bears part of the project costs itself (see Chapter 4.10). At the request of the government, this can continue to be possible on a project-by-project basis, with the proportion to be financed by the pension fund decreasing.

Furthermore, a citizen with additional contributions can assign these directly to a project. This corresponds to today's crowd funding on the free capital market. However, the citizen cannot choose a maximum return, but only a meaningful investment that is important for him.

The basic amount from the countries, which was put at €10 here, comes from tax revenues of the respective government. From these basic contributions, citizens may also make investments outside their country. However, it must be ensured that the tax revenues of the government, which the citizen does not allocate, flow into programs with investments of the paying country. The votes of non-voters are used for this purpose. The following numerical example is intended to illustrate this:

A country X, for example, has 30 million citizens and the basic amount would be corresponding to its GDP instead of €10 only €9 per month. Accordingly, 270 million basic deposits flow into the pension fund. If 20 million private individuals are non-voters, 180 million € remain, which the government distributes and reduces by possible pension payments (see 3.10). The government uses a distribution key to determine the projects into which the money is to flow. The capital requirements of the projects concerned are reduced accordingly. The 10 million voters can therefore decide on €90 million.

For a country in which no participant chooses, i.e. 100 % are not voters; this means that the entire basic amount of the government is distributed according to its budget planning. Two important consequences are worth mentioning. On the one hand, all projects must be transparent to the public and be processed, and on the other hand, these amounts give rise to a pension entitlement that can be understood as an additional basic security for the citizen.

3.10 Calculation example of the capital to be distributed monthly

With the calculation method presented here, the monthly capital available for distribution consists of the actual inflows, i.e. the state remittances per citizen for the consumption pension, the additional payment provided by private individuals <u>not</u> assigned to a project, and the repayments or cash inflows from projects. The regular pension payments and the annual payments to private individuals, the general costs as well as the part directly allocated to the projects and pensions by the non-voters via their state must be deducted from this.

In the following summary two countries pay in, with €12 respectively €3 as basic contribution. After the distribution of the non-voters, i.e. the allocation by the government or additional pension benefits (see below), 40 and 20 million voters remain. Of these, 3 and 1 million voters, respectively, have permanently assigned their votes to a project. (see also 5.1 Exemplary example).

	Voter in Mio.	**Basic amount per participant in EUR**	**Amount in Mio EUR**	
Country 1	40,0	12,00 €	480	Mio €
Country 2	20,0	3,00 €	60	Mio €
Total voter / basic contribution of countries	60,0		540	Mio €

plus additional payment by private individual not assigned to a project			20	Mio €
plus repayments (projects, investment income)			60	Mio €
minus pension payments			35	Mio €
minus costs			15	Mio €
Total inflows and outflows			30	Mio €
Free capital to be distributed in current month			**570**	Mio €
Results in a value per vote of	**3,17 €**	**resp. each voter**	**9,50 €**	

Let us now take into account the votes assigned as obligatory

Country 1	40,0	12,00 €	480,00	Mio €
Minus voters with mandatory vote	3,0	12,00 €	36,00	Mio €
Country 2	20,0	3,00 €	60,00	Mio €
Minus voters with mandatory vote	1,0	9,50 €	9,50	Mio €
Remaining voters	56,0		494,50	Mio €
Inflows and outflows as above			30,00	Mio €

Free capital to be distributed in current month for the remaining voters			**524,50**	Mio €
Results in a value per vote of	**3,12 €**	**resp. each voter**	**9,37 €**	

First, the value of a vote/voter is calculated without taking into account the mandatory votes. In the above example, one receives an amount of €3.17 for the value of a vote.

The figures are fictitious and chosen in such a way that for country 1 the basic contribution is higher, for country 2 the basic contribution is lower than the amount calculated for one voter. For the voters of country 1, therefore, the amount of the basic contribution of €12 is used, for the voters of country 2 the average amount of €9.50 is used for the obligatory votes. Thus the obligatory amounts are always at least as high as the basic contribution of the country or as the average value if there were no obligatory votes. The remaining free capital is divided among the remaining voters and amounts to €3.12 per vote or €9.37 per voter.

If a vote can no longer be assigned because, for example, the selected project was financed and released, blocked or deleted for political reasons, this capital flows into the project with financial character.

The liquidity of the pension fund is usually guaranteed, as there are always projects that have not yet been fully financed and released.

For additional payments by participants who have already reached retirement age, pension payments are due immediately. These additional benefits cannot therefore be fully allocated to projects. Depending on the age of the participants, the mortality table at hand and the experience gained from project returns, a part of the pension payment is required directly. This part therefore corresponds to a pay-as-you-go system of additional benefits directly into pension payments. The experience of life insurers can be used to determine the size of these amounts.

In the above figure example, the pension payments are lower than the returns from projects, i.e. from "money printing machines", repayments from projects with a credit character and the returns from the project with a financial character (investments).

If, however, the pension rights exceed the capital reflows from the projects and the shares from additional benefits, the pension payments are covered by the basic contribution, which the non-voters allocate to the government for distribution. First, the capital freely available for current pension payments is allocated as a percentage of the pension entitlements. The missing amounts are deducted from the non-voters' capital by each country for its pensioners. This leaves less distribution mass at the disposal of each government. Thus the different pension systems in the EU countries are not affected. The amount of the payment from the pension fund of monetary democracy is an additional, capital-covered pension contribution.

If the basic contribution of the country is not sufficient for these pension payments, the government concerned has to pay the pension payments additionally from its normal national budget. It can then no longer support projects. It makes far more sense to increase the basic contribution, i.e. the part of the national budget over which its participants can determine themselves. This also increases the capital of non-voters. This continues to finance the primary goal of monetary democracy, climate and environmental policy. In emergencies or critical economic situations, a parliamentary resolution can be passed to resort to the project with financial character and the shortfall can be offset by selling shares. In such a case the responsible representatives of the EU should check the budget of the EU country concerned for compliance with the rules according to the Maastricht Treaty, see also 4.17 'Public budgets'.

3.11 Linguistic diversity in the European Union

The European Union consists of 28 states and even more ethnic groups with different languages. For example, the Basque language (Euskara), this is spoken by about 750,000 people. Scottish Gaelic is an official language in Scotland and is used by about 150,000 Scots. In Catalonia, besides Spanish, Katalan and Aranese are official languages. This diversity must be preserved.

The transparency of the projects requires standardised data entry masks in the EDP, which are to be translated into all European countries. Thus 'remote Brussels' shows proximity to all citizens and respects local cultural differences. This standardisation reduces the translation effort considerably.

Additional free texts for a project should be written in the locally spoken language and in the European 'official languages' in order to receive votes and money from all European countries. The same rule is also recommended for feedback in interim and final reports, as provided for by transparency.

3.12 Access to internet

Not all citizens in the European Union have access to the internet at home. This is where public access can be created at public offices. It is also technically possible to check access via mobile phones.

3.13 State guaranty of additional benefits

Banks advertise shares with the hint that the purchaser becomes co-owner of a company. In the case of currency devaluation, one would still have a share of real assets. However, a company only has the potential to make a profit and to assert itself in the market. In fact, large corporations can become insolvent and disappear from the market. Their brands, such as AEG or Grundig, are still familiar to everyone.

The government warranty corresponds to the well-known inflation-hedged government bonds. Here, too, the investor is a co-owner of the state's infrastructure. This creates framework conditions and thus has the potential for companies to generate profits and pay taxes. All tax revenues are profits of the government, which benefit the population through government expenditures.

The difference, however, is that a company can 'disappear' completely. Employees have to find another employer. If, on the other hand, a country goes bankrupt, the population suffers, as has been seen with Argentina and Greece.

The conditions for repaying the extra benefits in monetary democracy are comparable to the conditions that Greece received during the euro crisis, i.e. lowest or no interest and a very long time horizon for repayments. Monetary democracy is thus a market-conform instrument for stabilising government units. It is an independent system and can mitigate the negative consequences of uncertainly financed election gifts or failed investments by government institutions.

4. Basic views: Why monetary democracy?

4.1 My democracy which I see

I am happy to have been born into a time and region in which peace reigns, and into a country that has placed human dignity as the supreme principle in the Constitution. A country that protects human rights, freedom of the press and social security for its citizens. A country whose government is determined by proportional representation and forces the political parties to cooperate. In order to be able to justify the topic and initiate a discussion at all, I ask myself the fundamental question: **What is democracy?**

We know that democracy is derived from demos and kratos, a rule of the people. I approach the concept of democracy with various quotations:

Francis Fukuyama[11], says: "An important message, therefore, is to understand that democracy does not include an infinite guarantee, even if it works well. A democracy is a complex entity, an institution that is at the service of a society that is predominantly in favour of democratic values. If, however, this structure shows weaknesses, democracy will also be shaken." ... "We all strive for efficient and reactive governments that respond to the demands of the population ... people want freedom. They want to decide for themselves and that is the real basis for democracy."

The philosopher and sociologist Geoffroy de Lagasnerie speaks in the same source: "Democracy is the only system that cannot be defined. To be precise, democracy is something that is never there. Democracy is something that is not tangible and of which one does not know what form it will take. ... because democracy is the only political system that carries within it the idea of a future, the idea of a critique of renewal".

And the philosopher and Sorbonne lecturer, Sandra Laugiers[12], has a similar expression: "The point is to make it clear to us that democracy is first and foremost a demand and as such always implies a form of dissatisfaction with the means of expression available to us. Democracy is therefore not an eternal guarantee of freedom, but an opportunity to fight for it again and again. If we do not, we lose it. From a perfectionist point of view, it must be said that ultimate democracy will never be achieved".

Thus my democracy, as I see it, includes freedom of opinion, freedom of assembly and the free press, which was consolidated in Germany by the Spiegel affair in the 1960s.

According to Polybios, there are two pillars of Greek democracy, one is equality before the law and the other is equal access to public speech in the Agora, which basically corresponds to today's idea of equality. The second pillar is the freedom to speak the truth: Parrhesia is an act of free openness and firm conviction. The opposite of charming eulogy and flattering art of seduction. Parrhesia requires courage, for speaking the truth is not entirely harmless for the speaker.

This leads me compellingly to the concept of civil disobedience. Since democracy is not an eternal guarantee of freedom, one must fight for it and thus disobey rules and laws.

The philosopher Sandra Laugiers says: "But what is important in all actions of civil disobedience since the 19th century is their collective character. The fact that we initiated a public debate and the players were not interested in themselves and, of course, the fact that they were non-violent".

In every association of people there are proposals for change, in dictatorial countries one speaks of resistance. Democracy creates a paradox. The political system gives rules, laws and freedom to the people at the same time it carries civil disobedience as an essential element. This structure of democracy must not, however, show any weaknesses in order not to be shaken. Historically, this has led to the separation of powers into the executive, legislative and judicial branches.

Triggered by developments such as the Brexit, the Pegida movement in Germany, the populist nationalist movements all over the world, the electoral successes of Trump and Erdogan, the undemocratic structures of the European Union, a debate arose about the stability and effectiveness of our democracies.

In the discussions and contributions, apart from laudable exceptions, the problems of the free market economy and financial capitalism are treated as an independent phenomenon independent of the political system. This could be because the political systems of Soviet communism, national capitalism in China or oligarchy in (some) Eastern European countries contradict our self-image of a liberal democracy. The fact remains for me, however, that a sufficient economic supply of the population is a premise of freedom and democracy. For me, the economic system thus becomes an elementary part of a political social order and shapes human consciousness and thinking for decades (see Chapter 4.14 and Chapter 8).

In the following chapters I will deal with various areas which, in my opinion, have developed negatively in recent decades - and which will experience an improvement with the introduction of monetary democracy.

4.2 Social market economy

The opportunities for everyone to become independent, to compete with others, to produce their products or offer their services have contributed significantly to our prosperity. The social components, such as the free trade unions, the social laws or laws on environmental protection, have made it possible to this day to create an environment for everyone in Germany or Europe in which everyone can develop freely.

The European Economic Community, today globalisation, combined with technical progress, has allowed companies to establish their production facilities abroad - in low-wage countries with lower environmental protection standards. We benefit from the goods and at the same time we find out in the media under what conditions people have to work or the environment is polluted. Microplastics are one example.

Every business enterprise, like every human being, has an instinct for self-preservation. I justify this statement with the fact that humans work in the enterprise and secure their economic existence by salaries and wages. A bankruptcy of a company has serious consequences for the life of every single employee. However, capitalism as a system sees insolvencies as something natural. In the USA this has led to the principle of 'hire and fire'. In European culture this idea is frowned upon.

This instinct of self-preservation on the part of commercial enterprises leads to employees taking over the essential goals of the owners: maximising the profits of the investors. In this way, every effort is made to influence the environment in which they operate - and thus also politics.

This instinct for self-preservation is also evident in companies that pursue non-profit-oriented tasks. As an example, I mention the waste water associations in Germany which, for a variety of reasons, prevent decentralised waste water disposal[13].

The organisation of an economic location is determined by the policy by means of legal regulations, an all-encompassing infrastructure and subsidies. Companies are therefore forced to influence politics in such a way that it creates framework conditions that support their economic activities. And the communities court companies to create jobs and tax revenues.to achieve this goal, politics is influenced by lobbyists. Since lobbyists have been dealing with a particular issue for a long time, they are ahead of parliamentarians. Through talks, invitations to events, legally drafted bills or the threat of job losses, and not to forget: Corruption - an effective system of lobbying has developed. Well-funded companies are far superior to NGOs and medium-sized businesses. This creates an imbalance that endangers SMEs and democracy.

The success of early globalisation led the director Donald Kendall of Pepsi Cola to characterise his power in an interview as early as 1974 with the following words: "I don't think we will see international trade unions or states or any supervisors, as I call them, manage to control a multinational corporation".[14]

The negative effects of a free market economy are obvious, including pollution or exploitation of people with inhumane working conditions[15]. The use of resources with an excessive consumption in the industrialised countries leaves oversized ecological footprints on the earth.

On the other hand, there are efforts by a minority to finance projects that do justice to today's tasks. But they are subject to capitalism. If, for example, a new wind farm is planned, around €100 million will be required[16]. The return of capital in this system must of course be calculated in such a way that it can compete with other financial assets. This also implies a much shorter depreciation period than the wind farm can supply electrical energy. If we look at the energy turnaround globally, a poor state will not be able to raise the financial resources for environmentally sound growth.

This is where monetary democracy comes in. Money is generated that goes into a country like money from development aid. This results in longer repayments and thus lower monthly reflows.

4.3 Overburdening the politicians

I'll start with a young person who has ideals and ideas. At school he experienced his talent, that he can convince others and that his ideas are put into practice. The ability to simply reflect more complex contexts, persuasiveness, oratorical and rhetorical talent are all useful qualities. If he finds himself exposed to criticism, he has to put on a rough skin. Shitstorm and personal insults that go below the belt have to drip off like a Teflon pan.

I remember very well the shadow cabinet of Mrs. Dr. Angela Merkel's first election campaign. Prof. Paul Kirchhof presented a concept for a necessary and sensible tax reform. The incumbent Federal Chancellor, Mr. Gerhard Schröder, dubbed Mr. Kirchhof ' a (perfect stranger) Professor from Heidelberg'. Mr Kirchhof left the shadow cabinet shortly afterwards. So a politician needs more than intelligence.

If a politician is elected to a parliament, he must convince colleagues who have the same talents and abilities as he does. As a party loyalist, he has to represent the party programme, even if not every point corresponds to his own values or is easy to understand. After all, he is a professional politician and his own existence also depends on being high on the party's electoral list.

If topics are concerned which affect the economy in their actions, then the innumerable lobbyists approach the parliamentarians. Lobbyists have often had draft laws ready for printing drawn up by relevant law firms. A well-formulated example researched by LobbyPlag can be found in Wikipedia[a] on the creation of the European Basic Data Protection Regulation.

The confrontation with different 'expert opinions', in which the client pays for his desired result, overtaxes the politicians. Decisions on conflicting theories of science become even more difficult. The Nobel Prize winner Robert Schiller advocated the view of behavioural economists that human beings decide not only rationally, but also with - casual - feelings. It was awarded to Eugene Farmer, a representative of Homo Oeconomicus, i.e. a rationally decisive human being. Quote: "Depending on which of our qualities or abilities economists believe in, their recommendations change"[17].

---

[a] https://de.wikipedia.org/wiki/Datenschutz-Grundverordnung

Politicians come into further conflict situations when fundamental convictions, beliefs or dogmas (see Chapter 8) influence a decision. One example is nuclear power, which in the early 1960s focused on the argument that without nuclear power the lights would go out. The different governments pursued different goals during their legislative periods. Decisions once made are justified decades later and are then revoked - and in some cases accused of being political. The establishment of commissions is also only of limited support, as several alternatives are often presented. This is also to be expected in the Coal Commission, which will present its results at the beginning of 2019 on the phasing out of lignite.

As members of parliament, they are representatives of their own constituency. In this area, they are the contact persons for citizens and functionaries such as mayors. Here, too, the work of persuading people about nationwide politics must be processed and local issues taken up and introduced and enforced in parliament. Often the concerns are connected with infrastructure projects and thus with funds.

And the world progresses: in technology, in the politics of other countries and always new, current topics such as diesel scandal, security and election manipulation in the network, etc. If we add to this picture the private tasks that the family, for example, brings with it, it goes without saying that political decisions by politicians cannot always be objective.

Of course, decisions are also prepared in ministries and by government Secretaries and thus also voted on in terms of content. In these parliaments, which are divided by interests, quick and effective decisions are rare. Monetary democracy can assume part of the responsibility and thus relieve parliamentarians.

4.4 Financial capitalism

For thousands of years, the owners have ruled over the majority of people and have determined their possibilities in life. Since the introduction of money, the proverb 'money rules the world' can be described as a basic principle.

Let's look at the relationship between the real economy, which produces cars, houses or services, and the global financial economy[18]: at the beginning of the 1970s the relationship between the real economy and the financial economy was still 1:1. There was a rule that money growth corresponded to economic growth[19]. In 1990 the ratio was 2:1, in 2013 it was 3:1. Now, in 2018, the financial economy with assets of almost 300 trillion USD is 4 times as big as the real economy with about 80 trillion USD.

I have three questions:

- What has this led to?
- How did this happen?
- What can be done against the dangers?

The first well-documented speculative bubble in economic history is known as the 'tulip mania' in the second half of the 16th century. On the stock exchange, bets were placed on the price increases of the tulip bulbs, which had become a collector's item. The world economic crisis in the 1920s was caused by a 'rush' of the population. Everyone believed they could get rich in a short time by buying shares. The 'black Friday' (it was a Thursday and there were several 'black Fridays' on the stock exchanges[a]) led to the world economic crisis and in Germany to hyperinflation.

[a] See Wikipedia

To demonstrate the power of the financial market, I recall September 1992. Quote: "The American hedge fund manager, George Soros, and multi-billionaire had bet on the collapse of the overvalued British pound and helped by throwing billions of pounds of previously bought pounds onto the market"[20]. The British government could not prevent the decline of the British pound with various measures and had to withdraw from the European monetary system, the prepared system for the introduction of the euro.

The true power of the financial market was illustrated in a computer simulation created by Swiss researchers in 2007, which graphically depicted the inter-relations of the economy. The so-called super cells hold shares in the largest corporations and play a key role in their economic policies[21]. Almost 40% of the total assets of globally active companies depended on 147 companies in the network. Very complex interwoven box companies are interdependent and the term 'system-relevant' became necessary. During the crisis of 2008 the real economy was dragged along and billions of taxpayers' money was raised to support systemically relevant financial institutions.

With the invention of the computer and sophisticated algorithms, financial transactions are largely automated with the aim of maximising profits. The asset manager BlackRock has the supercomputer Aladdin. Here the differences in the area of milliseconds between two deals mean who makes profit or loss.

Capital investments by the financial sector in corporations inevitably have an influence on the policies of all countries. At VW, for example, the Qatar sovereign wealth fund holds 17 % of the ordinary shares. One has a representative on the Supervisory Board and then talks concretely about VW's future policy. At the German bank, two representatives of the ruling house of Qatar are major shareholders with a combined 10%. With another representative from China, who also has 10%, they are so to speak decisive. With BlackRock of 6 - 7%, all three alone have 25%

shares in Deutsche Bank. Thus, the business policy of Deutsche Bank is mainly thought out in Doha / Qatar[22].

The countries themselves need tax revenues. It was not only in Europe that interstate competition arose as to which locations corporate headquarters should be located at the most favourable tax location. This conflict within the European Union continues to smoulder and solutions are being sought to collect taxes in the countries where the services are provided.

The global inter-relation of the financial sector is also being used by private individuals to avoid taxes. It is not just mailbox companies and numbered accounts that should be mentioned here. Even who is assessed for tax is different worldwide: the main residence and predominant residence or the nationality, as in the USA. The lack of tax revenue amounts to billions of euros.

Financial capitalism has got out of hand and is threatening the financial system of countries. The power of money influences the direction of big industry and, with the help of lobbying, it influences national governments. A tax avoidance system accelerates the opening of the gap between rich and poor.

The second question was how it could come to this. After the 2nd World War the Germans had no saved assets, since each received 20 DM during the currency reform. The economic miracle, which was mainly financed by bank loans, resulted in a distribution of income among the working population. Craft enterprises and the self-employed in various sectors produced a wealthy middle class. Over the years, capital was invested in life insurance and other securities.

A capital market developed in Germany that could generate money with money. The asset companies aimed at maximum profit and created securities of the most complex kind. With bets on price fluctuations, not only of stocks, but also of commodities, currencies and food, large profits could be made. Those who did not jump on this bandwagon not only missed their chances, but also endangered their own existence as asset managers in competition. Andreas Öhler, Professor of Finance, University of Bamberg[23]: "If a lot of experts talk in one direction, when it comes to economic forecasts, questions about how interest rates will develop, and they do so long enough, then more and more experts will incline in the same direction, as one can very well scientifically investigate. In the end, everyone does not want to be left with a "contrary opinion".

The speculation and wagering on future prices and the invention of new complex securities with bundles and reinsurances, mutual incitement with very high bonuses, led to a kind of "addiction of bankers". In Germany there is with gambling the reference: 'Game participation starting from 18 years, gambling can make you addicted.'

The 2008 financial crisis, originally caused by President George W. Bush Jr.'s announcement that every American should own a home, brought the financial system to collapse. Strong fiscal regulations were introduced, especially in the USA, and bank stress tests were carried out in Europe.

After the financial crisis, in which the countries had to support the banks, the government crisis came. Addicted adventurers from uncontrolled shadow banks immediately wagered on the solvency of entire countries, e.g. Greece.

In order to minimise the dangers, the ECB floods the capital market with an ultra-expansive monetary policy. Prof. Helge Peukert, Prof. for Financial Economics and Sociology at the University of Erfurt speaks[24]: "...that the glut of money has the same effect as that oil is poured into the fire".

There are contradictory recommendations as to how the danger represented by the experts can be countered. There is talk of a full-money system, a ban on short selling, the introduction of a financial transaction tax or the restriction of pre-frequency trading.

So we have reached the third question of what can be done. Politics has been made known with a wide variety of possible solutions and approaches. However, every internationally active politician has the obligation to represent the interests of his own country. The necessary unanimity in the European Council also prevents the introduction of effective instruments and tax legislation throughout Europe.

It was only 10 years after the financial crisis of 2008 that on 3rd/4th December 2018, after 18 hours of negotiations between the European finance ministers, there were improvements in the stability of the financial market. The European rescue fund ESM will be increased with € 60 billion and is to become the European sovereign wealth fund. Hopes for the introduction of a transaction tax were not fulfilled. This shows that the matter is very complex and is assessed differently. The issue of the stability of national budgets and the currency of the euro shows how difficult and protracted the unification process in the European Union is.

Monetary democracy has an international dimension. With a democratic, responsible and acting education of young people (Chapter 4.14) I expect a shift in values in the long term and across generations. Monetary democracy will withdraw money from asset companies and life insurance policies, but not to the extent that their existence could be jeopardised. Since life insurance companies also have difficulties in investing capital profitably because of the ECB's expansive monetary policy, they can see monetary democracy as an opportunity for the future (Section 6.2). Nevertheless, I expect great contradiction from this power structure of the financial world and quote Heinrich Heine (1797-1856) from his winter fairy tale:

"Money changers, bankers, you even have

whipped out of the temple -

unfortunate dreamer, now you're hanging on the cross

as a warning example."

4.5 Infrastructure

Already at the beginning of the 20th century there was a lack of money in the public budgets to let the broad population participate in the technical developments. As an example, I would mention the electricity supply via electricity grids in the city of Berlin. Here, contracts were concluded with private investors who still enjoy the protection of their property today. Today, the infrastructure in Germany is to be financed through PPPs (Public Private Partnerships). Although these are limited in time, they are costly for taxpayers and future generations.

In France and Italy, people were under the illusion that with the construction and management of motorways by private hands, everything is regulated and the public budget is relieved. In both countries, assets are being redistributed from the bottom upwards. In Italy, as demonstrated a few months ago by the collapse of the motorway bridge in Genoa, safety is not guaranteed either. There are also shortcomings in the road network in Germany. At the Rhine bridge near Schriesheim[25] a pillar moved. There were cracks and the bridge had to be closed. The investment backlog with road and bridge reorganisations is enormous. President Trump also wants to invest billions in infrastructure rehabilitation in the USA.

Austria took a different path. The motorways belong to a state motorway company, which can finance the maintenance and (partly) the new construction through tolls. The annual surpluses in the millions flow into the Austrian government. This can be seen as a project of monetary democracy. The motorways belong to the state, i.e. the people, and the surpluses go back to the people. The focus here is not on maximising profits, but on a functioning infrastructure, as demanded by the monetary democracy.

With the construction of the Gotthard tunnel, Switzerland and Germany signed an agreement to extend the Rhine Valley railway line between Karlsruhe and Basel. Nothing has happened in Germany for more than a decade. We do not know the reasons for this inactivity. With monetary democracy, the rough planning of the route can already be introduced as an independent project. It cannot therefore be due to the financial resources. The monetary democracy also has solutions for citizens objections, e.g. to noise pollution. Delays can be reduced by an additional construction of a sound barrier, which is financed by the mere vote of the citizens concerned.

The infrastructure also includes the connection of all households and companies to a well-functioning and fast Internet. German politicians have been trying for years to connect rural areas to the broadband network. It is precisely the free market economy, which has been so successful, that has ensured that politics has produced a strange situation, as outlined in point 5.4 as an exemplary example.

The supply of drinking water and sewage water is not the focal point, but just as cost-intensive and necessary[26]: "Waterworks throughout Germany have to invest billions to renovate an outdated, dilapidated sewer system. Consumers are asked to pay for an outdated system. The legal basis is the obligation to connect to the public sewer system that has been in force since 1935. These are operated and maintained by sewage water associations. Alternatives for small villages, such as local bio-treatment plants recommended by experts, must be fought for in court - and the connection to the sewage system is nevertheless subsidised by the EU. The head of the Sustainability Institute in Potsdam, Prof. Töpfer, former Environment Minister, compares the costs of the sewers with the fact that "we take the sewage water to the sewage treatment plant by taxi".

How can monetary democracy put an end to this nonsense?

In monetary democracy, subsidies are distributed by the people to Europe. Transparency can lead to an enlightenment that prompts politicians to reform outdated laws such as those of 1935. Not only the citizens concerned, but also the public authorities are grateful for such local bio-sewage water treatment plants because of cost savings. The instinct of self-preservation, which the special purpose sewage associations possess as a company, must be regulated by an empathetic solution between the politicians and those affected.

In the long term, the monetary democracy system will have more and more influence on the expansion and maintenance of the infrastructure.

4.6 Difficulties of retirement pensions

First we ask the question how the world should look like for older people who have shaped today's world through their life's work:

1. A life-affirming environment

   This is granted by a country that lives in peace and freedom. It has a functioning infrastructure with the supply of food, doctors, care, communication, mobility and a clean, non-toxic environment with an adapted climate.

2. A well-functioning economy

   It is always the working population that has to finance and care for the children and pensioners. But in order for the economy to flourish, a life-affirming environment is a requirement.

3. A sufficient income in retirment

In Europe, there are very different pension and ageing-security systems. In the Netherlands there is a sufficient basic pension. In Austria, government pension entitlements are much higher than in Germany. Using the example of the German old-age pension system, I show similarities and dangers.

a) The government pension (inter-generation contract)

Our population pyramid shows that fewer and fewer people in employment have to finance a pensioner. Not only in Germany, but also in Austria, this system is reaching its limits. Necessary reforms, which politicians must carry out at regular intervals, only secure pension payments for a limited period of time. The last reform in Germany is only valid until 2025. In some countries, such as Norway, a pension fund is to defy these dangers.

There is already poverty among the elderly in Germany today. Many pensioners buy food from social institutions (so-called 'Tafeln') and go to the social welfare office, a humiliating walk in my opinion. Now, before the election campaigns, a basic pension is being discussed.

b) Property

Property is a real existing asset such as residential property. This means that there are no running costs for rent and can be sold if required. It is a result of the private life achievement.

c) The company pension

By means of laws and regulations, it is possible in Germany for employees to agree a contractual company pension with their employers. The employee and the employer each pay part of the regular contributions. This system is voluntary and very unfair to those who do not have a permanent job with a company. Furthermore, it is a coincidence in which company one works and receives more or less company pension entitlement. The company Fleischmann had to apply for insolvency because the claims from the company pensions could no longer be generated. The small self-employed, the 'I-companies', the temporary workers or those who do not fulfil the operational conditions due to a change of job (as it is the case with me) do not receive anything from this regulation.

d) The funded pension

This pension is built up with savings plans or one-off payments and is subsidised by the government. In some countries it is mandatory. The investments are life insurance policies, equity funds or other securities. Until a few years ago, investors could not choose what asset management institutions do with money (see Chapter 4.11). Asset managers invest with the principle of profit maximisation and not in sustainably producing companies. The following paradox has arisen as a result of developments over the past decades or centuries:

People save for a pleasant retirement. Their savings flow into profit-oriented companies that constantly destroy the foundation for their own human life on earth - the life-affirming environment.

Monetary democracy is a complementary social system: concrete participation in shaping the present and future as well as additional financial security in old age.

4.7 Referendum yes or no

Democracy means 'the rule of the people' and is often legitimised by means of a referendum. In addition to the legitimacy of a decision, voters also feel that they can decide about their own country.

The vote in Ireland on whether or not an abortion should go unpunished has a different dimension. The majority decides how an individual can behave. A woman is unintentionally put in a desperate situation for herself because her culture does not offer her an appropriate solution. All she has left is to have an abortion abroad.

The values of a society have grown through traditions and religions and are subject to temporal changes. In Germany, women took to the streets protesting against abortion paragraph 218 and forced politicians to change criminal law. Even in the case of euthanasia, politics in Germany presumes to determine criminal regulations of a moral nature. Although an ethics commission was included in the debate, the person concerned is forced to travel to Switzerland or Belgium in order to escape his suffering. In Germany, politicians are afraid to divide the people with such questions. This is what Health Minister Spahn calls the search for a compromise on the ban on doctors advertising abortions. I feel incapacitated as a citizen. In the following chapter 4.8 further developments of democracy are presented, which in my opinion can become an important European instrument for such topics.

Referendums are customary in Switzerland. The decision to build the Gotthard Base Tunnel was positive here. This referendum is (almost) a blueprint for monetary democracy. It was voted on a part of the national budget. It was voted in favour of an infrastructure construction which, in the long term, would represent a 'money printing machine' and would immediately have a positive impact on rail and road traffic.

On the other hand, the construction of new mosques was rejected in Switzerland. Here another advantage of a referendum comes to light. Foreign policy can now ban investors from building mosques without any loss of face on the part of the government.

Monetary democracy is a kind of referendum, i.e. a direct participation of the people in government affairs. It is no longer necessary for a majority to decide, nor for a majority in the parliaments. However, the majority has the right to prevent or delay controversial projects and developments. It is a new means of direct democracy and reduces the political influence of profit-oriented companies and large investors.

4.8 Proposals for further development of democracy

The philosopher, Mr. Rainer Forst, employee of the Frankfurt Excellence Cluster 'Normative Orders'[27] describes the situation in our society with the words "...there is a feeling that democracy no longer works". He concludes: "We must find a new policy, new forms of politics". He justifies these statements with elites who are out of touch, alienation, globalised capitalism, that nobody cares about their own people. As a professor of political theories, he sees a worldwide triumph of authoritarian, nationalist parties or figures. As examples he calls the election of Donald Trump, the Brexit or the election in Brazil and summarises this development with the English term 'take back control'.

There are suggestions for developments from various fields.

The Chinese philosopher Tondong Bai refers to Confucius: "Everyone has the potential to become a wise and compassionate person - in reality only a few can achieve it". He proposes a two-chamber system, a lower house whose members are directly elected by the people, and an upper house. This should include people with special intellectual and moral abilities, an elite, who could, for example, have prevented the Brexit.

Jason Brennan, a professor of political science at Georgetown university in Washington[28], describes most voters as hooligans: "People who see politics as a 'we versus the others', incapable of making sensible decisions. As a solution he envisages a change in electoral law: "Not everyone should have the same right to vote. Those who are more informed than others may cast more votes.

In Germany the Federal President supports ideas for strengthening democracy with the 'Forum Bellevue zur Zukunft der Demokratie' (Forum Bellevue for the future of democracy). In various cities there are developments which have a positive effect, e.g. the participation of citizens in Filderstadt or the ISEK programme.

The Republic of Ireland has chosen a different path[29]. About 5 years ago, citizens' meetings were convened in which randomly selected citizens discussed political issues and proposed solutions to the government. In conservatively Catholic Ireland, gay marriage was discussed in such citizens' meetings. This public and active participation of the voters led to a referendum in which the gay marriage could be introduced in Ireland without large demonstrations of the opponents. At the same time, in France, the government from above was fighting through gay marriage. The result: rage on the streets. The participation and the co-determination as well as the influence, so a member of a citizen assembly in Ireland, is the best what could happen to him. Experts are said to have calculated a model for the EU as well.

There is seldom anything in the press to be read or heard about this kind of democratic development. Prof. Dr. Rainer Mausfeld quotes John Dewey[30]: "Political competence is a collective attribute that arises from the possibilities, the free, open and well-informed discussion of a community, i.e. political intelligence depends on the public debate room being intact. ... As long as secrecy, partisanship, prejudice, misrepresentation, propaganda and sheer ignorance prevail in public education, there is no way to judge the political intelligence of the masses."

The question arises as to when and who will further develop a democratic structure. In historical, revolutionary events, such as the end of the war after the Second World War, new constitutions are drawn up which seek to eliminate the weaknesses of earlier constitutions. During the reunification between East and West Germany, the constitution of the Federal Republic of Germany was adopted with very few changes. During the development of the European Union, substantial rights were transferred to the Union; during the introduction of the euro, sovereignty over its own currency was also transferred. Despite the undemocratically organised institutions, I take a very positive view of the European unification process.

If democratic constitutions show weaknesses, constitutional changes which took place through a parliamentary decision or a referendum can destroy basic democratic principles. They primarily serve to maintain the power of the respective government and the claim to absoluteness that its world view must also have its people. These setbacks of democracy are visible in recent years in Turkey, Hungary and Poland.

Major deficiencies of a constitution, such as the separation of powers (separation of the executive, legislative and judicial branches) are rarely dealt with or not dealt with for decades. In Austria, the Czech Republic and Germany, the judiciary is not separated from the executive. In Germany, the judiciary and the public prosecutor's office are subject to the authority of the Ministry of Justice. This despite the experience of the Nazi era, during which the judiciary was 'brought into line', and although my knowledge in the GDR was based on the same regulation of 1877 unjust judgments[a] [31]. Only in Great Britain did justice reform take place between 2003 and 2009.

Technical developments can also offer approaches for further developing democracies. To my knowledge, the right to vote with electors was introduced in the USA, as the size of the USA made it difficult for the people to vote directly. Although it is known that it is not the president who receives the most votes from the people who becomes president, there is no initiative to change the electoral law there.

In Germany, constitutional changes are 'easy' to make when it comes to scarce money. In chapter 6.3 I describe the inclusion of the PPP in the constitution. On the occasion of the 'Digital Pact', the Mediation Committee discusses how the federal government can provide direct funding for the tasks of the regions (status 12/2018).

Monetary democracy is a supplement to existing government orders. I therefore do not see any insurmountable legal difficulties in the individual countries in Europe. In the complex structure of the European Union, however, unanimous solutions by the heads of government are necessary. The European Parliament has no right of initiative. Active citizens must therefore be found who together as a group generate pressure and attention, so that a steady introduction of monetary democracy can begin, as outlined in Chapters 6.1 to 6.3. Support from the press is essential.

[a] www.gewaltenteilung.de

4.9 Situation in Europe

Europe has evolved over decades from the mining treaties to the Roman Treaties, the European Economic Community, the European Community and today's European Union. To forge a union whose individual member countries have the most diverse cultural backgrounds, the most diverse social systems and forms of government, which have experienced wars and hostilities in centuries, is a mammoth task. The network of government institutions between the European Council, the European Commission and the European Parliament is not easy for people to understand and is criticised as undemocratic. Unanimity in the Council of Europe is an obstacle to effective politics. Through a large bureaucracy, incomprehensible laws, such as the degree of curvature of a cucumber (meanwhile withdrawn), create resentment and distance of the people to Europe.

The European Union wants to counter this development. An Internet survey was conducted in 2018 on the abolition of summer time. The response from the population was minor. For the change of year 2018/2019, an Internet presence was created by the European Union: www.what-europe-does-for-me.eu. Here the interested citizen experiences the influence of the European legislation on the daily life. The funding programmes are also presented. It is a flood of information in 24 languages. I wonder who has the time here to inform himself as a 'normal' voter. Monetary democracy, on the other hand, actively calls on everyone to determine their own life by means of a vote. This active approach to voters binds them more to Europe than elections to the European Parliament.

The accession of our eastern neighbours to the EU after the collapse of the Soviet Union did not bring prosperity for all, as the countries hoped. Capital with the principle of profit maximisation brought new ownership and undermined the goal of equal living conditions for all citizens of the Union. Individual states turned away from the European Union and found new sources of financing in China (see 4.22).

Today, freedom to travel within Europe and the single currency in the euro area are taken for granted. Other positive projects, which are only made possible by European subsidies, disappear in an overall assessment of the European Union by citizens.

In public, negative headlines get more resonance than positive news. When the term "madness in the billions" is introduced by the press into subsidy policy, the negative feeling towards Europe is reinforced. More on this in chapter 4.10.

The European Union is called a community of values. A strong, neutral element binds the European Court of Justice here. It has been achieved, for example, that the early retirement of constitutional judges in Poland has been revoked. Nevertheless, there are statements that foreign regulations come from remote Brussels, which one does not want to introduce. With the principle of subsidiarity, citizens hoped to preserve their identity and a high degree of autonomy. The statements of local politicians that negative developments come from Brussels are very problematic. If one could decide for oneself, things would look better in one's own country. Unfortunately, in the election campaigns in Germany there was no detailed topic that focused on Europe[32], as former Foreign Minister Joschka Fischer formulated.

Monetary democracy, on the other hand, will change the feeling for Europe and bring together the most diverse European peoples. Every citizen can see which projects are implemented in his local environment and can decide for himself. Such a system does not exist in any country in the world. This experience of being able to directly help shape the inactivity or opinion of one's own country's government will significantly change the cohesion and unification of Europe. This can also deconcentrate the intricate responsibilities in Europe between Parliament, the Council and the Commission. The dispute over membership dues, which Mrs Thatcher, as British Prime Minister, took to the top and pushed through special arrangements, will disappear.

4.10 Subsidies and appropriation

There are various types of subsidies. Permanent subventions protect, for example, an industry such as agriculture or enable a socially acceptable reduction of jobs, such as coal subvention. Research facilities and laboratories, even if operated by industry, receive project-related subsidies. Politicians have also decided to establish new industries, such as Airbus or the European space industry ESA. These and similar subsidies are not affected by monetary democracy.

The subsidies and grants to be replaced by monetary democracy have the basic idea that self-participation is necessary for a project to be financed and implemented.

In the Bonn area, along the motorway and 500 m away from the nearest apartments, a children's playground was built with subsidies - in nowhere. Local politicians criticise the chaos in the planning of various offices. However, they took advantage of the favourable opportunity to receive subsidies from the government and on the one hand considered what else we could offer here for children. However, the residential area project had lost sight of it[33]. The project as a residential area is now being tendered and something should 'happen' in the year 2020 to 2022.

This kind of 'shotgun approach' of giving money to regions in order to improve living conditions there does not only promote senseless projects. In the broadcast 'Milliardenwahnsinn'[34], corruption and abuse are denounced. Therefore it is also made clear that the current subsidy policy is inefficient. Abuse becomes clear when subsidies are awarded for a wellness park in the Czech Republic for a multimillionaire or in Germany for a hotel complex where the person responsible is now in custody.

Or like the famous railway bridge over the Elbe in the Czech Republic: the EU has paid a good €33 million for a modern lifting bridge for three-storey container ships. The problem is that there are no 3-storey container ships in Czechoslovakia; there is no shipping traffic. The bridge has not even lifted in 7 years. Nor can it, because the rails have been welded tightly. Gold plated EU millions - the Czech authorities are to blame[35].

MEP Inge Gräßle, together with other MEPs, checks what happens with subsidies on behalf of the European Parliament[36]: "What I very often see is the classic waste of money, where you carry out a project that you really should not have carried out; where you carry out a project that, on sober consideration and closer inspection, no one really needs".

The inefficiency is also confirmed by the European Investment Bank. The Fact Sheet 4-Environment-de on the Juncker Plan (as of 2015) reads: "Despite the considerable efforts of the Union and its member states, bureaucracy and government complexity in the EU are being reduced too slowly and unevenly. This is a particular problem for SMEs (small and medium-sized enterprises). The strategy used today can be seen in the Investment Plan for Europe (European Strategic Investment Fund EFSI). This is intended to correct market weaknesses by covering part of the default risks of investment projects with public funds, and to further mobilise private and public funds[a]. Although sufficient liquidity is available, promoters are not in a position to tackle their projects. Investors are over-cautious because the regulatory hurdles are high "...and further "EFSI is endowed with € 21 billion, € 16 billion comes from the EU budget and another € 5 billion from the reserves of the EIB (European Investment Bank). This will allow the fund to trigger additional investments of at least €315 billion over the next 3 years".

This document, dating from 2015, received the following comment on 23.09.2018 in the news programme 'Tagesschau': "European subsidies of €270 billion are not called upon, among other things, because the own contribution cannot be raised or projects were not planned.

The above explanations clearly show the undesirable developments of the European Community. Bureaucracy and government complexity' and 'regulatory hurdles' prove the lack of transparency and the alienation of

[a] www.eib.org/about/invest-eu

the European institutions from the population. The distribution of subsidies in the hands of national governments promotes corruption instead of preventing it (see Chapter 4.19). Monetary democracy, on the other hand, is transparent and based on the rational decisions of collectively voting population groups (Chapter 2.7, penultimate section).

If we look at the broadband expansion in rural areas in Germany, there has been a great oversight in the last 10 years. The Federal Government provides funds, the EFSI has stated as its goal 'strategic infrastructure' in the telecommunications, transport and energy sectors, in particular interconnected networks and urban development.

The examples given here show the inefficiency of subsidy and subvention policies. There are enough papers, books and film reports on this topic.

Politicians must learn that investors are only interested in their own profits. This is a necessary objective for SMEs, which have the most jobs in the European Union, to survive in competition.

Subvention policy is such a complex system that even consultancies have been able to establish themselves to help interested parties obtain justified investments.

Monetary democracy does not have private investors such as life insurance companies, asset managers, etc. It assumes that smaller companies or private citizens, community councils and NGOs want to implement concrete projects that are also accepted and desired by the population. It is therefore a matter of promoting sustainable projects quickly, non-bureaucratically and effectively. The introduction of monetary democracy will have only limited funds available, so that an adjustment process to the existing national and European funding pools can take place slowly. The aim is to replace as much as possible the ineffective subvention policy in Europe and in individual countries with monetary democracy.

4.11 Capital market for retirement provision

The way people deal with money is very different. One wants a big car, the other does without it and wants to save money for his pension. Another saves for a house, the other for times of need. According to these needs, there are many different possibilities on the capital market: building saving contracts for one's own house, securities such as government bonds with little price fluctuation for times of need, temporary savings plans at banks such as a driver's license account for children, shares or life insurance as an investment for topping up a pension. Speculative securities to increase one's own income.

Monetary democracy thus competes with existing forms of capital investment for old-age provision. The following is a comparison of exemplary examples:

a) Life assurance

   As a rule, this is a savings plan, which causes high costs at the beginning of the transaction. One-off payments are also possible, even during the pension period, whereby the pension payment begins in this way.

   In Germany, life insurance policies can be financially supported by the government in the form of capital-forming benefits or Riester contracts. During this term a notice and/or the access to the saved capital is possibly limited only, which corresponds to the monetary democracy. Pension payments are often dynamically contractually fixed, e.g. to the government pension level. In the current capital market, life insurers unfortunately cannot even compensate for inflation. I have to expect that my pension payments will only have half the purchasing power in 10 or 20 years.

   During the savings phase of the capital, a return of up to 7% should be achieved in order to be able to meet the investor's expectations at all. To this resolution, the funds are invested in different ways, some of which are regulated by law in sovereign wealth funds. Also pension funds and/or life insurances hand over the saved capitals to asset management companies such as BlackRock. There they expect a higher net yield than those, which they can gain themselves. Through the pursuit of profit, precisely those companies are now supported which, in competition, generate the desired dividends by foregoing cost-intensive environmental protection and climate protection, e.g. by relocating production abroad.

This is where the paradox arises that a 30-year-old father of a family makes long-term financial plans for his wife and children that destroy the environment for his children in old age.

With monetary democracy, the investor has the direct opportunity to control his money in such a way that he feels it flows there, so that in 30, 40 or 50 years it will provide an environment worth living in.

b) Equity funds

You can also invest money in equity funds in the form of a savings plan or one-off amounts. However, the equity fund is subject to greater fluctuations and is generally only recommended if you are looking for a long-term investment strategy. Among other things, passively managed index funds are recommended.

On 6 June 2018, the programme PlusMinus recommended Swedish old-age provision as a model for Germany[a]. In Sweden, citizens are obliged to contribute part of their income in a funded way. There are 800 funds to choose from. Otherwise, the state

[a] [a] https://www.daserste.de/information/wirtschaft-boerse/plusminus/sendung/hr/altersvorsorge-106.htm

takes the money and invests it in the state fund AP7, which has generated 9% annual returns over the last 20 years.

Those who speculate only on returns with equity funds have the same disadvantages with regard to environmental development as with life insurance.

There are already banking institutions such as Triodos Bank and others that are committed to ethical principles. There are also platforms in which projects are financed for which no credit is granted by 'normal' commercial banks. With the introduction of monetary democracy, sustainable funds will significantly increase their share of the total market from the current 2 to 3%.

c) Government bonds

Government bonds are securities that are subject to minor price fluctuations and must be used for capital cover in the case of life insurance companies.

The advantage of government bonds, equity funds and equities is that investors can sell the securities on the stock exchange at any time and become liquid accordingly. A stock price risk is always present.

d) Shares

After the big price loss of the so-called 'Volksaktie' (people's share), the German postal service, investors in Germany have less confidence in equity investments. Worldwide, however, there are many 'middle class rich people', which secure themselves an additional income from existing capital through the stock price losses. This phenomenon is to be seen with the middle class in China exactly the same as with pensioners in Europe. This kind of 'mixed financing' of the necessary life income requires a lot of knowledge about the stock market and the acceptance of price losses. This brings the management of securities into daily life. The same disadvantages apply to one's own old-age provision.

e) Gold and commodities

Gold is also frequently used as a capital investment and is subject to regular price fluctuations. Here, too, the focus is on the hope that gold is a safe investment and that it will also enable a materially protected life in old age.

f) Other securities

Among these I select securities that promise a high return. This promise attracts investors to invest in it because they are convinced (much-loved obviousness) that they can finance a secure retirement.

Again and again there are reports that windy business is made thereby and the investors run into the danger of losing their entire capital. If for the age precaution a total amount of 90,000 € was invested by Gisela S. with P&R[37], then one can regard this as not concerned as frivolous. P&R has sold containers as an investment, rented them to freight forwarders and promised the depositers a buy-back after 5 years. In recent years, P&R has sold containers to 54,000 investors, who have invested a total of around €3.5 billion in the company from Grünewald near Munich.

Years ago, PROKON promised high returns of 10% and more with wind power plants. The investors saw on the one hand this net yield, thus the faith much money - secured age, on the other hand an alternative, in order to support energy production without environmental load. As known, PROKON went bankrupt and the investors were able to take over the already installed wind turbines and formed an association.

These two examples show that there is a lot of capital available that needs to be invested. Essentially, it is savings from their own lifetime achievements or through inheritance cases that the parents were able to generate during the time of the economic miracle in Germany. In this respect, I assume that, when monetary democracy is introduced, large amounts of capital will flow into the pension fund as additional benefits.

Monetary democracy is perceived in exactly the opposite way. The money is safe, it works across generations and you will enjoy your well-deserved retirement.

g) Ownership with right of use

Relatively new is the sale of one's own home with a lifelong right of residence. The advantage here is that people in old age no longer have to worry about their assets, but can focus on their well-deserved retirement. The investment product of monetary democracy satisfies precisely this clientele with the addition that they know what their money is used for.

The statement in Chapter 4.4 can be repeated for the capital market that is the determining factor today:

People save for a pleasant retirement. Their savings flow into profit-oriented companies that constantly destroy the foundation for their own human life on earth - the life-affirming environment.

Monetary democracy is an attractive competitor in classical financial capitalism. In addition, there is an expansion of the population's mentality that capital can be used not only to maximise profits but also to shape the world in conjunction with self-interest.

4.12 Efforts to achieve autonomy in individual regions

In 2017 / 2018 Spain and Europe were influenced by the autonomy movements of Catalonia. In Romania, too, the Hungarian-speaking population, the Szeklers, want to achieve autonomy. In the examples, cultural identification, including language, is accepted by the central government.

In interviews with demonstrators, the argument that one's own economically prosperous region has to donate money to the central government without profiting from it is repeated again and again. This is perceived as an unjustified confiscation, whereby it is also assumed that the central governments do not handle the money properly and sensibly.

Monetary democracy can have a satisfactory effect here. Citizens can allocate funds to an autonomy movement in their region. Supporters and opponents of autonomy can also be within a family. Conflict situations become rarer as a result of a secret vote, as voting must guarantee in monetary democracy. Through the presentation of all projects it can also be seen that funds from other countries or regions flow into a concrete large-scale project. This solidarity connects different regions with the institution that introduced monetary democracy. The same reasoning applies to the growth of the member states in the European Union.

4.13 Foreign und development policy

For centuries, international politics has been determined by the pursuit of power, economic interests and ideologies.

In the Cuban crisis of 1961, the blocks of the USA and the Soviet Union faced each other. They wanted to expand their spheres of influence, be it through a world revolution of communism or through capitalism.

In the Middle East the peoples had to endure much suffering for decades until today. After the end of the First World War, the Sykes-Picot Agreement established countries such as Iraq and Libya on the map with the ruler alongside the colonial era. In the 1930s the groups from Mussolini marched into Ethiopia and the emperor Haile Selassie felt left alone by the League of Nations. The development of Syria after the Second World War was bloodied and war is still raging there today. It is therefore understandable that the confidence of these countries in the Western world, politics and culture has been destroyed.

The term banana republic stems from the fact that large corporations from the USA covered climatically preferred regions and countries with monocultures. This economic power has led to a corrupt elite and poverty among the population in the affected countries. Nicaragua is still struggling with the consequences. Even today, big business is being courted and called upon to do so by international institutions. Quote[38]: "This not only gives capital, i.e. large scale industry, major corporations, the power to dominate a banana republic, a cocoa republic like the Ivory Coast of Ghana, as before, but even the official seal that they must strive for it".

China's foreign policy wants to avoid the mistakes of Western and Russian diplomacy[39]. A second Syria should not be repeated. China is self-confident and it is well known that China has a foreign policy that includes a win-win function (see chapter 4.22).

If we look at energy production in Poland or China, it is essentially determined by coal combustion. Other emerging countries intend to build new coal-fired power plants, such as Bangladesh. In the USA, Trump wants the old coal mining areas to flourish again. These national interests stem from the politicians' responsibility to ensure that their own people are well off and that everyone can share in the prosperity.

Monetary democracy cannot influence conflicts due to religious-ideological motives. The conflict between Iran and Saudi Arabia postulates itself in the cruel proxy war in Yemen. Ukraine's efforts to achieve freedom led to military action by Russia, so that the Crimea was annexed and peace has not yet been established in Eastern Ukraine. Monetary democracy has no influence in such conflicts, but can become a model for international cooperation.

There is no form of government in the world, be it a democracy or a dictatorship, be it national capitalism or a kingdom, capable of guaranteeing a satisfactory infrastructure anywhere in its own country. Knowing this well, international agreements have to be made with the ruling party, even if they do not satisfy human rights.

Monetary democracy is not dependent on the goodwill of governments. It is based on the needs of people who are supported by other people; see e.g. 5.8, sewage treatment plant in India.

4.14 Education and training

I In Germany, the call for education, training, education is ever-present. On the one hand there are complaints about the lack of teachers, on the other hand there are complaints about the school buildings, some of which are in unreasonable condition or the lack of computers and access to the Internet. In the second case, monetary democracy can have a direct impact, as illustrated by a way of example in 5.1 for a bridge.

In core, the issue here is educational content. In the 1970s, my school discussed the extent to which humanistic education is necessary for a fulfilled life and, on the other hand, how to meet the needs of the economy in such a way as to facilitate entry into professional life. Then we have free schools, such as the Waldorf Schools, which focus on people. History has shown us that humanistic education could not prevent either the First or the Second World War. Therefore, further contents have to be communicated to the children and young people in order to preserve our democratic values.

In the curricula and the working groups there are offers which bring the young people closer to democracy. There are courses on the culture of conflict, there is the student co-administration, there are youth parliaments in communities. The philosopher Rainer Forst, who works in the Frankfurt Cluster of Excellence 'Normative Orders'[40], says: "Yes, democracy cannot exist, so that even in the early phases of life, in all the social institutions where children grow up, democracy is learned. This has something to do with tolerance, with solidarity, with a whole series of attitudes that have to be practiced. But it also has something to do with the sense of justice ..."

Mr. Wolfgang Thierse and Prof. Dr. Norbert Lammert, both former members of the Presidium of the German Bundestag, agree that democracy includes conflict, i.e. the struggle for the best solution. The author Heinz Buder, whose books on the state of the German soul and German society are classics of sociology, also says[41]: "I think we need in Germany ... more controversy about the fundamental questions of our future".

Mr Wolfgang Thierse says[42]: "The expectation that democracy will fulfil my many desires for prosperity and security directly and quickly cannot be fulfilled by democracy. It is precisely because democracy is a dispute that lasts between different opinions. That requires patience, an appalling amount of patience ... we know from history that a dictator can be quick, that everyone else pays the bill".

So if young people learn about the culture of conflict, attitudes and patience, then the teaching in vocational schools looks different. In training companies the basics of capitalism, i.e. profit maximisation and competition, are trained in a practical way. Again and again, there are competitions for young people and trainees in cooperation with companies to find out how they have to behave in the free market in order to achieve the greatest possible profit. In FINANZTIP's newsletter of 21.11.2018 it is announced that FINANZTIP, together with the renowned IZOP Institute, will provide more financial education for young people in more than 80 classes and courses nationwide. Every evening before the evening show in the 1st programme, the programme 'Börse vor 8' will be broadcast. In the schools there were teachers, who buy shares (also with pocket money of the pupils) and the pupils requested to study the stock prices. Every evening the students receive direct feedback and learn how to get rich with speculation.

In a survey of the headmistress and headmistresses conducted as part of the 2006 Pisa Study[43], it became apparent that "almost 87% of 15-year-old schoolchildren in Germany attend a school where business and industry exert an influence on the teaching content". And further in the same source: "...more and more companies, business associations, chambers of industry and commerce, employer-related foundations are pushing their way into the school's only sheltered enviroment. Alone 16 of the 20 highest selling companies in Germany now offer free teaching materials in order to convey their view of things to the next generation.

The young people of our society are trained to take up capitalism as their primary system, because money means prosperity and a happy life; democracy, however, means conflict and patience.

Decades of training in the successful system of the free market have an effect on politics and its decisions. I am not talking here about the advocates of the free market economy, but also about the solution approaches of critically thinking politicians. The introduction of the flat rate per case in the health care system, the private registration offices for implants or the private senior citizens' and nursing homes are characterised by the *much-loved obviousness* that the market regulates everything (see Chapter 8.9). This leads to the statement that the human being is there for the economy instead of the economy for the human being. Monetary democracy has <u>no</u> effect on the examples mentioned, as these are running costs. A long-term change in mentality will reveal other ways of realizing it.

Young people and adults will be confronted with the problem of climate policy, the infrastructure, some of which is in need of renovation, and in many places in Germany with a dead spot. In comparison to other countries, they see themselves as being somewhat dependent on each other - and should learn to be patient.

In the programme 'Frag den Lesch' (Ask Mr. Lesch) the thesis was put forward that the deniers of climate change had an ethics of the 19th century. People at that time only saw their individual environment, i.e. the community, the region and perhaps the country. They perceived only one or two generations, that of their parents and that of their children. A theoretical ethic for the global world and for unbelievably long times has yet to be developed.

Monetary democracy takes up exactly this topic, whereby the people themselves can act quickly and receive regular monthly feedback. If the projects and project realisations are presented through short films before the large news broadcasts, democracy gives the people a sense of responsibility and co-determination. I therefore advocate that pupils from the age of 16 should be made familiar with monetary democracy in schools. What astonishment will arise among the young people if their name is known to the government through the tax number / social security number. The new, democratically and citizen-oriented organized EU will allow and demand the young people to assign 10 € to a project and to be able to experience the realisation in real time. There will be a stronger feeling than the first voting card you receive after the age of 18 to take part in democratic elections. But it is more, it is an active participation in our democracy. It can be the basis for a 'theoretical ethics for the global world and for unbelievable long times'.

4.15 Relationship between people and politicians

The former president of the Bundestag, Dr. Norbert Lammert, defines the relationship between government and people as follows[44]: "The basic principle of democracy is that every power, every decision-making authority entrusted to anyone must be traced back to a decision of the sovereign people and all their members".

Mr. Wolfgang Thierse confirms that the ballot box is a very precious basic principle of our democracy[45] and continues: "Democracy must live with ignorance, with stupidity, just as it must live with arrogance and impudence, impertinence". Even if the words "ignorance" and "stupidity" have been chosen unfortunately, this could be one of the reasons for the following evaluations, as they are used in an interview in the programme Kulturzeit[46]: "For more and even more the democratic system becomes a mirage, mock debates, transparent election campaign manoeuvres, placebo-controlled discussions and always the others are to blame. (Politicians) avoid clear words in order not to become vunerable. They talk the way they talk because they don't trust the voter to deal with content. Instead of becoming committed democrats, voters become consumers of well-packaged advertising. Our image of democracy is the result of decades of conditioning. Is the political elite systematically educating its citizens to become minors? Seemingly clear solutions, seemingly clear politics. This is the core of po-pulist successes, like a fever that also affects established parties. Irrational offers of identification that hardly anyone wants to believe. From elites who have always claimed to educate the people. At the ballot box 10 Germans are more important than 5".

The philosopher Svenja Flaßpöhler is editor-in-chief of the philosophy magazine and comments as interview partner as follows: "...that this relationship between elite and people, a very, very difficult balancing act, really decides the success of democracy". She explains the two extremes with the Spanish philosopher Ortega y Gasset, who said that "the people are stupid and seducible by populists ... and therefore elites must protect the people from this seducibility ... But the other way of thinking is what we are currently experiencing and what the Causa Maaßen shows, namely that the elite are taking the people for idiots, i.e. that the people are very stupid, and that the elite considers the people are actually ... a very serious problem that we have to struggle with today".

Mrs. Flaßpöhler points out 3 points which she sees as the solution to the current problem:

First point: "A government that wants to enjoy the trust of its citizens must show courage ... it must adhere to ideals ... a radical decision at the right moment."

The second point she interprets in the concept of trust: "Of course the people must trust the elites. That's perfectly clear, but conversely the elites must also trust the people, in the maturity of the people. Elites must not treat the people like stupid children, but they must trust in the maturity of the citizens".

The third point is education.

If I consider the enormous pressure that politicians are under, the complexity of the tasks to be solved, which a single person cannot grasp at all, then Mrs Flaßpöhler's second point must be emphasised. The elites, the politicians, must have confidence in the decisions of the people.

Konrad Adenauer has expressed the view that politics is successful when it can simply present complex interrelationships.

In political elections in representative democracies, politicians are forced to offer simplified answers. Voters, however, base their electoral decisions strongly on personality and the catchy arguments that give them a positive feeling: 'This man, this woman, can improve my personal situation'.

Perhaps the relationship of politicians to their own people is shaped by the words of Hannah Ahrendt: *"The effectiveness of propaganda demonstrates a main characteristic of modern masses: they believe in the invisible, in the reality of their own experience, do not trust their eyes and ears, but only their fantasies. What convinces the masses are not facts, not even invented facts, but the consistency of illusions".*

In the election of US President Donald Trump, it was revealed that the British software company Cambridge Analytica provided voters with certain information about the new media. One concealed negative statements of the own candidate and placed negative statements and events of the opponent. Of course the successes of the own candidate were emphasised. The whole thing was supplemented by so-called 'fake news', which were obviously refuted. The truth of Hannah Ahrendt's statement is evident from the number of citizens who stood at the Capitol during President Trump's swearing-in.

Monetary democracy opens up an additional opportunity for the population to make and influence simple decisions themselves. The voter knows exactly what is important to him or herself: a bridge, a fast Internet or a sewage treatment plant in India.

The confidence of politicians in the people can be broadened even further. There is a wide variety of expertise among the population that monetary democracy will have access to. The transparency that must be made public for every project will enable interested experts to exercise a control function that is not possible with parliamentary means or public prosecutors.

4.16 Public budgets

Since governments have existed, public budgets have been chronically underfinanced. I think there are several reasons for this. Public funds are used directly to provide people with financial security through social benefits. An infrastructure is being set up to guarantee a decent standard of living and economic activity. This includes internal security, the educational system, the administration and the legal system, as well as roads and water supply, etc. The funds should be sufficient for this. On the other hand, there are misspending's such as those revealed in the Black Book by the Bund der Steuerzahler or the Bundesrechnungshof. As explained for subsidies, see chapter 4.10, due to existing financial structures and the fact that they *much-loved obviousness*, useless but effective projects are implemented.

The financial crisis in 2008 devoured an unimaginable amount of taxpayers' money to support the economic system of neoliberalism. A collapse would have meant unimaginable destructive consequences for the real economy.

The Maastricht Treaty introduced criteria to prevent over-indebtedness. With the introduction of the euro, governments had to learn not to counter budget deficits with excessive monetary policy.

The Swabian budget rule 'one spends only the money one has' or the proverb 'save in time, and you have when in need' was never observed. The economic regulation according to M. Keynes is that the state reserves money when the economy is doing well in order to combat a weakening of the economy was ignored. With tax revenues going well, 'gifts' were and are given to the citizens, because the next elections are always on the agenda.

Monetary democracy is a system that uses tax revenues effectively and will reduce tax squandering. In relieving the burden on public budgets, care must be taken to prevent further social gifts to citizens on a debt basis. It could be that the Maastricht criteria for a new debt of a state have to be tightened and adapted.

4.17 Overtraining of humans in today's world

Do you belong to the group of people who have already changed their electricity provider? Or do you belong to significantly more than half of the Germans who, according to a Bitkom survey, have never changed their electricity provider in their lives?

And if you belong to the first group, what tariff did you take? How did you check the seriousness of the provider? And how much time did it take you to find a new 'supplier'? Have you already changed your health insurance, your liability and household insurance, your car insurance? Are you sure that you have the cheapest mobile phone rate? Are you still a bargain hunter? Do you drive from one supermarket to another to buy margarine for 13 cents less?

Can you understand your electricity bill or your pension award? And what about your funded pension plan? Do you have endowment insurance, shares or gold? Or do you still believe in the Riester pension, which the insurance branch earns the most from? Or would you prefer to play it safe and build your own home, most of which belongs to the bank? Have you really chosen the most favourable long-term financing?

- ✓ **Capitalism needs attentive market participants**

Technological progress has changed our world - and requires our full attention. As helpful as a smartphone may be, as every day the use of a PC seems to us, we also have to protect ourselves against endangerments. Be it the 'data theft' or viruses and Trojans. And factory 4.0 comes with the AI. Are you really firm in it?

- ✓ **Technical progress challenges us to**

And what do we hear from politics and the news. The climate change, the financial crisis, terrorism, Kim Jong-Un in North Korea, Trump in the USA, Syria, Iraq and Afghanistan. Can you process and understand all this spiritually? Do you recognise narratives (see chapter 8.5)? And then populists threaten a shift to the right, a nationalism in Europe! Which party can you choose, which politicians can you trust? And which news do you believe? Can you distinguish between 'truth' and 'fake'? Are you affected by the diesel scandal? Is the limit of 40µg NO_2 right or is it safe to exceed it, as the report 'Das Diesel-Desaster'[47] convincingly points out? Do you know: if a person hears a statement again and again that he accepts it as correct? Do you also respect contrary opinions? Do you trust our politicians? How do you deal with the flood of information?

- ✓ **Democracy is a gift that needs responsible citizens**

Donations help in crisis areas, but where can I help most effectively? Volunteering is praised and used, be it for the food banks or during the wave of refugees. Am I more in favour of animal welfare or environmental protection? As a 'little person', can I have any positive effect at all? Or do you leave everything to the government, the churches, the non-profit associations, therefore 'others'?

- ✓ **A community needs commitment**

Doesn't your work require full concentration? Do you take work home with you? Are you reachable privately for the employer? The work with which we earn our daily bread demands full concentration. Do you suffer from a burnout or do you already have the widespread depression? Are you afraid of unemployment or poverty in old age? Are you in temporary or permanent employment? Is your company doing well?

- ✓ **The job demands: In the sweat of your view...**

And living - be it in the family with partner and children, be it as singles, be it to have time for a hobby or in a club - don't you want that too? Don't your pubescent children worry you? How do you deal with the responsibility for your family? Are there useless arguments in the family? And then come the fees, incomprehensible laws and rules, taxes that make the rich richer and the poor poorer. Will their money last until the end of the month?

- ✓ **People set priorities for their individual lives and forgive themselves if they have never changed their electricity provider**

The many negative reports in the press, not only about climate change, but also about corruption, subsidy deception, overpopulation, etc., can create a feeling of helplessness in individuals that can lead to feelings of despair. Here I transfer Prof. Dr. Klaus Lamm's[48] statement about the suffering of others: "There is a natural protective mechanism to not always expose oneself to the suffering of others ...". So it is not morally reprehensible to do this in principle and that we have this ability."

Today's situation reminds me of the times of the Cold War. To have to imagine that the earth could be destroyed by nuclear missiles had to be suppressed at least temporarily in order not to endanger one's own life. The majority turns away from it.

- ✓ **Democracies are in danger - they need an update!**

Monetary democracy relieves the burden on citizens. You can have a say in your own environment from your home PC. For old-age provision, the capital market and its dangers can be pushed to the sidelines. The information is no longer 'fakes'. With girlfriends and friends you can do something large without having money yourself.

Monetary democracy connects individuals with common tasks.

4.18 Media / Press / Debate room

The press and the media constitute the public room for debate[49]. They are at the mercy of market laws and pay attention to the circulation strength of their newspapers or the ratings on television. The press selects. Prof. Dr. Rainer Mausfeld on this: "Public opinion is no longer a free room for discussion, but something that is shaped by an entire industry".

The printed products are directed substantially at certain target groups. The topics are limited to what the readers want to read. In the case of television programmes, there are documentaries whose topics often only shed light on negative, critical developments. It seems that positive reports result in lower ratings.

Monetary democracy also needs investigative journalism. Democracy itself also needs a public room for debate. In order to bring about a change of mentality, as already demanded by monetary democracy for young people, a process of retraining the press seems necessary. How this can be shaped in concrete terms is a task that public broadcasting in

Germany has set itself. One example is the introduction of theme weeks, which offer different perspectives under one term (e.g. justice). I do not have any documents on the effectiveness and success of this format.

In November / December 2018 there were protests in France called 'Yellow wests'. It was not a classic demonstration organised by trade unions or other firmly established institutions. No, the population used the technology that we Europeans enjoyed during the Arab Spring: the social medias. The extent to which the social networks can provide an appropriate room for debate, also with a view to monetary democracy in the future, can be influenced by the designers of democracy.

4.19 Against corruption

Romania will take over the Presidency of the European Council in 2019 (effective from the beginning of December 2018). In the run-up to the presidency there were accusations of a lack of fight against the corruption that prevails there and of restrictions on the independence of the judiciary. The accession countries in the Balkans, such as Albania, Serbia and Montenegro, are also suffering from corruption. This is a major obstacle to the accession of these countries to the EU.

The EU's efforts to date to bring the candidate countries into line with the EU's rules and requirements seem to have failed. It is feared that open borders will make the people there very willing to leave the country. It was pointed out that the Balkan countries would then become the least populous countries.

With the EU's subsidy policy being converted to the criteria of monetary democracy the ruling classes will no longer have any money at their disposal. The swamp of corruption from direct EU funds is drying up. Local corruption in the construction of projects can only be reduced to a limited extent. However, the population itself experiences through its own initiative that local tasks that can be solved through projects are directly financed and supported by the EU.

4.20 German basic law amendment due to digital pact

Federalism in Germany has transferred educational sovereignty to the federal counties. The budgets of the federal counties are underfinanced, so that the education sector also lacks funds for necessary investments in the digital sector. This is to be remedied by the so-called Digital Pact, in which the federal government makes money available to the provinces. However, this can only be done with an amendment to the Basic Law, which requires the approval of the majority of both parliaments. While the Federal Parliament approved the draft law, the Federal Council (representation of the counties) unanimously (!) rejected the draft law. Main criticism was the mixed financing, that for each EURO of the federation also the country must grant an EURO and the fear, that the Federal Government can intervene into the sovereignty of the counties. The Digital Pact is not explicitly mentioned in the Act, but the amendment to the Basic Law is also intended to promote other infrastructure measures, such as the expansion of local public transport. In mid-December 2018, the law was referred to the Mediation Committee.

This example makes it clear to me how encrusted a system is and how it persists in its inertia. Politicians want to decide what makes sense and what is good for the population.

Monetary democracy is taking a different path. The population, local councils and parliaments know what is necessary for the population. The sovereign, the people, decides and rationally finances the various proposals. The people regain sovereignty.

4.21 Public procurement practice

The procedure for awarding public contracts provides for a Europe-wide call for tenders. Offers must have been received by the Authority by the closing date and the contract must be awarded to the lowest bidder. The public itself is not briefed.

In Germany, practice is such that the cheapest is not necessarily the cheapest. Supplements are often required for larger properties. With smaller orders also the degree of popularity of the regional company plays a role: one knows oneself, trusts each other and makes it.

The Elbphilharmonie and Willy Brandt BER Airport in Berlin experienced major difficulties during the construction phase. The Elbphilharmonie had different skills, and Berlin Airport had serious planning errors. After taking office, the Lord Mayor of Hamburg, Mr. Olaf Scholz, relatively quickly transferred the award of the contract to a group of companies, which then implemented the project quickly under its sole responsibility, incurring considerably higher costs.

Abroad, the German companies can deliver on time after good detailed planning, as an Olympic stadium in England shows. In the Netherlands, deadlines are set for the completion of motorways, with bonuses being the rule for earlier completion and reduced payments for late completion. Construction delays are therefore rare in Holland.

The practice of awarding public contracts has not proven itself in Germany. Around 2014, a working group was set up to draw up proposals for improvements. I do not have any results in this respect.

Monetary democracy should fall back on the results of this working group. However, the conventions of today's public-private partnerships must be abandoned: "The contracts are usually secret and the state is often misused as a scourge for investors".[50]

4.22 China – my geopolitical perception

The data of the following paragraph were published in 2015[51].

The environmental impact of large cities in China has been known worldwide since the Olympic Games. Since 2007, more carbon dioxide has been emitted in China than in America. China had the highest CO2 emissions in the world. 77 % of the primary energy consumed in China came from coal. The enormous economic growth, development and waste of energy had the result that 50 % of the world's coal production is now burned in China. In the cities, smog alarms are declared, e.g. in Beijing in 2013 on 60 days, in Xingtai, a city with 7 million inhabitants on 129 days, i.e. for more than 4 months. In addition to the burning of coal, the rapidly growing car traffic is also a cause of environmental pollution. It is estimated that car traffic accounts for 25% of Beijing's fine dust emissions. The proportion of PM 2.5 particulate matter in China is higher than anywhere else in the world. Water pollution from acid rain and direct pollution is also obvious. In China, water pollution is the main cause of protests and demonstrations in several major cities before air pollution. The population can express their displeasure by showing signs to the local environmental authorities. The number of these ads rose from 300,000 in 2000 to over 700,000 in 2010.

In recent years, the Chinese government has taken effective action against this negative development with the system of what we call national capitalism. Drones are used to measure industrial plants. If the values exceed the prescribed limits, there are fines that would have been unimaginable just a few years ago. China is well advanced in the field of e-mobility and is not only praised for this by the German Minister for Economic Affairs, Mr Peter Altmaier, but also regarded as a strong competitor of the German automotive industry. To the best of my knowledge, China is a leader in the installation of new wind farms and solar plants. To the best of my knowledge, there is also a strict policy against corruption.

These figures show that global climate protection is only possible in cooperation with China.

On the other hand, China's international policy must be taken into account. After the sale of the KUKA Group to Chinese investors in February 2018, the then German Foreign Minister and Vice Chancellor, Mr. Sigmar Gabriel, warned against the Chinese geopolitical advance[52]: "The initiative for a new Silk Road is not what some in Germany believe, a sentimental reminder of Marco Polo, but it stands for the attempt to establish a comprehensive system for shaping the world in the Chinese interest. This has long ceased to be a matter of economics. China is developing a comprehensive system alternative to the Western one that, unlike our model, is not based on freedom, democracy and individual human rights."

On the other hand, European cohesion is not sufficiently consolidated by common ethical values. Subsidies are not sufficient to bind poorer countries to the European Union. In Greece, Hungary and Serbia, China has already gained a firm foothold and, as in Australia and more than half of the African states, is trying to achieve domestic political decisions in its favour. When Portugal was in the financial crisis, Chinese capital helped them overcome the economic crisis. The French president Macron had to hear this from the Portuguese socialist president when he wanted to introduce takeover protection for European companies by foreign investors. In December 2018, Germany went it alone and decided that foreign investments in German companies could only amount to 10% instead of 25%. This will reduce the number of sell-outs.

Monetary democracy will strengthen the European Union in the long term. (Strategically important) infrastructures, such as the port of Piraeus, will no longer be readily sellable. Sufficient capital will be available for new infrastructures. It will be more difficult for other countries to impose their image of humanity on us with money.

5. Exemplary examples

5.1 Bridge will not be built over 13 years

The bridge on district road 30 between Dalberg-Wendelstorf and Cramonshagen has been closed by the district since 2005 due to serious damage[53]. The responsible county only wants to repair the damage if the government pays half of the costs. The subsidies are to be provided in 2019 / 2020. To date, there has been no response to the application.

The following scenario is likely for monetary democracy:

Legally, the cost bearers (county, communities) accept the financing with the monetary democracy and jointly determine who the client will be. In the local press the difficulty is reported and the citizens are called upon to assign the basic contributions cumulatively to this project.

Let us take the following numerical example: A new bridge costs €1 million and 5000 participants of the monetary democracy assign their monthly basic contribution of the state of 10 € to this project. Thus €50.000 per month are accumulated, so that a full financing is reached after 20 months.

If further 100 participants have a savings plan in the pension fund, then they can assign without paying attention to net yield, their contribution also to this project. If the amount is 50 € per month, another 50,000 € per month will be collected, so that a full financing is already achieved after 10 months.

If the assignment is assigned by the participants mandatory (see chapter 2.6) up to the full financing this project, then the start of construction can begin with a planned construction period of ¼ year already after 9 months or earlier, according to the planning of advance payments. This time is sufficient for the preparations that the executing companies have to make.

In this concrete case, in monetary democracy there are no competence problems with the responsible institutions, no application management for subsidies and, as can be seen from the figurative example, no rapid repair of a necessary infrastructure.

5.2 Urban development

With the ISEK[a] programme, the Federal Republic of Germany has made a very successful programme available to the communities under the Federal Ministry of the Interior for Building and Home Affairsb. Many municipalities use the federal and government subsidies and have drawn up their own independent plans.

For many years, Richard Sennett has been committed to urban development that is against purely investment-led interests. He wants to prevent the ever-increasing ghettoisation in our cities, keep it open, in the sense of a living cooperation. However, Sennett says[54]: "Real estate has long become the new security, tons of gold, Trump's father already knew this, is multiplying by putting a lot of pressure on urban planning with a lot of money and thus accelerating it. So Trump's father and his people forced many exceptions. The city government became his servant because they were afraid that New York would fall into disrepair without investments. So it comes to a sellout of the city."

---

[a] Integriertes Stadtentwicklungskonzept

[b] www.staedtebaufoerderung.info

The city of Pforzheim was destroyed by a bombing attack on 23.02.1945. Accordingly, real estate is from the period of reconstruction. For the eastern part of the inner city, a Dutch investor has registered, who has presented a concept with almost €100 million, which is supported by the mayor. After publication of the project documents, there is now of course strong resistance, which clings argumentatively to various points, such as traffic management.

Pforzheim is also one of those cities that was brought to the point of ruin by the credit business with Deutsche Bank, where the bank always wins. (More details can be found in the court files of the city of Milan against the Deutsche Bank.) A major investor seems to be a stroke of luck for the depressed financial situation.

If we compare this with the city of Filderbach with a citizen's participation and a responsible person, the city of Aachen, which is drawing up a 10-year plan and implementing this concept, or the city of Bretten, about which the magazine Brettener Woche of 18.11.2015 reported, then the suspicion suggests that Pforzheim is subject to a Trump - imitator. And this despite the fact that 200 metres away from a good shopping mile (Schlösslegalerie) lies a ruined shopping mile of the investor Steinhart.

Pforzheim is not an isolated case. In Homburg / Saarland an investor jumped off. Already in 2016 the excavators should roll, but again and again something came in between. Now a complaint of the neighbouring municipality St. Ingbert. A shopping mile with 80 shops was planned. The head of the town hall, Mr. Rüdiger Schneidewind (SPD), does not believe that another investor will come[55]: "Personally, I believe that it is too late now. A few years ago we would certainly have had the chance, but we read all the trade journals, read the normal media, the online trade has grown. It's getting harder to rent out the stores overall."

Mr. Schneidewind addresses the problem directly. There is a structural change in the trade. Connected with it is the task of the communities and cities to find a concept for an alive, worth living city. This requires ideas and the commitment of the citizens.

With monetary democracy, a scenario could look like this: Citizens, e.g. through citizen participation, and city councils define the space that can be redesigned. For the creation, they announce an architectural competition, which as rough planning is a project of monetary democracy and is financed accordingly. From several possibilities, the city council can now also decide in a municipal "referendum" which of the possibilities should be implemented. A new project for monetary democracy is detailed planning and time planning, which is also financed by the pension fund. The result of the detailed planning can now be given to the population for financing in batches, i.e. divided into time periods as individual projects or as an overall project.

With monetary democracy, it will also be possible for financially troubled cities to realise meaningful and qualitatively good urban development together with their citizens.

5.3 Wind turbines

Wind turbines are manufactured and operated by large groups such as EnBW, Innogy (a subsidiary of RWE) and cooperative companies.

Huge wind farms have been built in northern Germany in recent decades. Local landowners have thus earned good money in some cases. Such facilities can be counted under the heading of "money printing machines". Since the maintenance effort is low and the wind costs nothing, the conversion into high-quality electrical energy is cost-covering at any price - if the interest on the invested capital is omitted.

A new wind farm has an investment volume of almost €100 million[56].

With monetary democracy, it is precisely these costs of interest with a high interest rate that are eliminated. Even if the price of electricity was to be reduced or the EEG subsidies were to be completely abolished, a wind turbine would still be profitable to operate. Exactly this illustrates the approach of monetary democracy.

If the EEG levy is abolished, capital can be collected with the help of monetary democracy in order to install such not highly profitable but environmentally friendly plants. The property owners and operating companies apply only for the capital from the pension fund, which is necessary as a loan in addition to the equity capital. Thus the economic interests of the property owners and operating companies are protected further. However, there is no risk of no longer being able to repay the interest charges if the EEG expires or the fixed interest periods expire and a follow-up loan has to be concluded. For investments from the pension fund, only transparency is required, which must also be submitted to every investment bank.

5.4 Fast internet and radio holes in Germany

Fast Internet and optimal coverage for data transmission in the 5G standard is nowadays a vital infrastructure such as water, electricity and roads. It does not only affect the private supply, but in particular small and medium-sized enterprises, which can lose their competitiveness without fast Internet access.

On 25/26.11.2018 it became known[a] how the 5G implementation will be processed. The regulations for awarding the auctions for the necessary frequencies in spring 2019 stipulate that the purchasers are to erect radio masts in cities along motorways and railway lines up to country roads. National roaming is rejected by the major mobile phone providers Vodafone, Telekom and O2 with the words that it would amount to dispossession. National roaming would be such that in an area where 3 radio masts are necessary for coverage, each provider would build one and give access to the other. Bitkom also spoke out against a national roaming introduction, because it is expected or feared that nobody will then build a mast.

[a] German TV programme ARD / ZDF

In addition to the costs and the service that a mobile communications provider promises its customers, the greatest possible availability of room for customers is a competitive criterion. As things stand today, all three providers are building radio masts in cities, railways, major roads and motorways. In other words, hardware equipment that is 3 times too high. The customers who suffer are those who have to finance these investments.

The auction revenues for the confederative government will also be lower. Each of the bidders must also calculate in its bid how many investments are necessary for the required coverage with the 5G standard.

The dogma that the free market regulates everything has created an abstruse situation. The policy does not act after the specifications of the Basic Law that an equalization of all regions demands, but is subject to the dogmatic sounding sentences such as expropriation or 'that it is not a market economy'. These dogmas have become part of political thinking. End users therefore have to pay the highest mobile phone tariffs in Europe because their money is invested three times.

With the help of monetary democracy, the scenario could be completely different. Mobile operators themselves decide which cities and areas they want to guarantee full coverage. For the remaining areas, a public company will be set up to negotiate and supervise the construction of the necessary radio masts and the maintenance contracts with qualified companies. Financing can be provided through the pension fund on a continuous basis, also by allocation of state investments. It must then be agreed in the contracts with the mobile phone service providers that these radio masts must also be used. The increased fees that the mobile service providers have to charge for this are attributable to the state. In the case of an appropriate cost determination by the state, e.g. 1 € per month, a permanent "money printing machine" for monetary democracy is required.

With this solution, mobile operators will be able to offer higher auction amount. This amount could be used directly for the construction of the area-covering radio masts.

Even if this scenario is regarded as utopian, it becomes clear that the introduction of monetary democracy will create more options for politicians. They have more room to negotiate against powerful corporations and can thus better fulfil the priority of the Basic Law.

5.5 Highways

An essential aspect of the State's task is to provide the population with an environment that enables economic and private action. Financing in Germany via the fuel tax has not been sufficient to plan and realise new buildings sensibly, let alone maintenance. The integration of tolls for trucks has also caused difficulties for the operating companies. The German Minister of Transport, Mr Scheuer, announced an out-of-court settlement. Toll Collect still had to pay 3 billion EUR. However, this is only about half of what the government demanded. At the same time, there is a new tender procedure which is to privatise the company again from March 2019. Of course, the old operators have applied again.

The parliaments simply passed a constitutional amendment to Article 90, according to which public private partnerships required (see 6.3). It is time to consider changes to the system of representative democracy.

It is incomprehensible why the Austrian model cannot be introduced in Germany. Monetary democracy comes into action when investments are necessary, be it for new construction or for the maintenance of bridges.

5.6 Energetic renovation of houses

There exist subvension programmes for the energetic renovation of houses, i.e. thermal insulation and installation of more efficient heating, which are mainly based on low-interest loans.

The risk remains with the homeowner. There are, for example, heat pumping systems that were removed or shut down after one year because the electricity requirement was so high that conventional heating was much cheaper. The investments are thus put in the sand. The risk remains with the house owner.

With monetary democracy, the transparency of technical information is also present. Also the repayment of the costs of the measure takes place over a standardised evaluation of the energy saving. With this principle the "black sheep" on the energy market are sorted out. As initiator of a concrete energetic measure an union of smaller crafts enterprises can proceed with the monetary democracy from the ranges insulation, heating and installation, solar technology with reference to the qualification on house owners and go over all formalties for the house owners. This means in this case that with the project requirement it must become clear, how highly the actual energy saving is expected and a reflux of the spent capital can take place. The house owners, frequently also pensioners, have to bear only the annoyance with building measures. Their costs remain constant and follow only a general price development. For this program a central office is necessary, which takes up the appropriate data and charges the difference to be paid annually between the actual costs of the energy input and the calculated costs without energetic measures. This principle of repayment is common for the www.bettervest.com platform.

At the World Climate Conference held in Katowice in December, it was pointed out that of 50 of the most polluting cities worldwide, about 30 are located in Poland. A large part comes from the old heaters, which are fired with coal and wood.

Through the internationalisation of monetary democracy and a climate protection agreement on the basis of monetary climate policy taking into account efficiency, competitive heating systems etc. could be effectively distributed worldwide. This seems to me to be more effective than increasing funds in UN programmes for emerging countries, as the efficiency and control of the support programmes is uncertain.

5.7 Involvement of NGOs

NGOs (Non-Government Organisation) are associated and engaged worldwide. In addition to organising protests against the current political situation, they also support projects in various countries. There are also UN sub-organisations that pursue concrete projects of an ethical / moral nature.

Non-governmental organisations are internationally linked. They have direct contact to local problems and tasks worldwide.

Already today projects are supported and promoted like the preservation of the jungle as a CO2 sink, drinking water treatment plants, sewage treatment plants etc.. In addition to NGOs, the initiators are local activists and representatives of communities and towns.

Through these information sources, projects for environmental and climate protection or infrastructure measures can be submitted to the authority for the administration of projects.

The projects must, of course, be carried out in a transparent and legally secured manner. A look at the NGOs themselves could also be important to see to what extent the promised targets are actually met. I would remind you of the documentation "The Pact with the Panda" from 2011.[57]

5.8 Wastewater treatment plant in India

The collapse of the multi-storey factory in Bangladesh, where the clothes discounter KiK had sewn, has been continued in a court in Germany. This is the first time that a company in Germany has been sued for damages under Bangladeshi law.

Less well known are the consequences of leather production in India. It is important to us to have beautiful shoes, sturdy bags and soft purses made of robust leather material. In the tanning of the raw leather, toxic substances are used which are discharged untreated into the sewage water, e.g. in India[58]. The nearby river is a cesspool and it should be clear to everyone that the poisons are discharged into the sea. In the long term, we will also be affected, as the example of the microplastic or the Fukushima disaster shows, in which radioactive material was carried across the Pacific to North America.

With the help of monetary democracy, the following development is possible. Groups of environmental activists, the local council or a regional parliament submit an application to the Authority for Projects in Europe. The project would be a type of project described here as project support. In addition to the previously mentioned criteria concerning the environment and legal security, it must also be ensured that the maintenance and upkeep of a sewage treatment plant is borne by the community / region. The European peoples, i.e. the individual person can now decide whether a wind farm in the Baltic Sea is more important to him than a sewage treatment plant in India. After the complete financing of the purification plant the region receives the complete financing and the purification plant thus as present. So there is a win-win situation: The technology can be exported from the industrial countries, the local water can be purified in the shortest time and in the long run one of the thousands of inflows of sewage water with toxic substances is relieved. It is only a small part that does not get into the food chain, but this is exactly one goal of monetary democracy. Many small improvements ensure a cleaner environment.

5.9 Solar plants as development aid and foreign policy

As briefly outlined in Chapter 4.13, Foreign and Development Policy, the Middle East is unstable and has lost confidence in Western foreign policy. At present I see stable countries only in Jordan, a country in which the German Air Force is stationed, and a country that has taken in hundreds of thousands of refugees from the Syrian war. Tunisia, a country in which the economy suffered after the Arab Spring and where unemployment is high, is also currently struggling for internal stability.

With the help of monetary democracy, solar power plants can be offered in the form of projects with regular reflows or with interest-bearing repayments in order to stabilise the countries. This can be initiated by a European foreign policy or directly by companies. In such a case, money flows back into the pension fund. Contrary to normal lending, repayment is linked to actual income. One can, for example, agree that half of the local electricity price is set as the repayment amount. If the plants do not reach the predicted energy quantities, the repayment rate must be adjusted, in contrary to normal loans. The existence of the operator and owner of the solar power plant is therefore not endangered by a reclaim of the loan. For the pension fund, this only means that a repayment will take place for a longer time in a smaller amount. The reflows are used for new projects so that they cannot be co-financed as quickly as expected. The same reasoning applies to the pension entitlements to be financed from the returns.

This again creates a win-win situation. There are many different techniques for solar power plants: mirrors concentrate the light on an evaporator, on tubes with salt liquid or direct solar panels. The storage of electrical energy, which is not used during the day, can also be done using the latest technologies, be it electrolysis with the production of hydrogen, be it through the melting heat of the salt, be it through heat storage in special concrete. All these technologies are in competition and can be further developed and verified by large plants of the kind envisaged here. For the country itself, there is the most environmentally friendly electricity and jobs are created. This automatically leads to social stabilisation and an infrastructure for the local economy through the power stations.

For foreign policy this means a completely new approach. If it wants to actively support governments in a country, it must promote the relevant projects. On the other hand, if a state does not respect human rights in the way our people perceive them, then it will not provide funding for such a project. An essential "lever" of international politics is transferred to the people, whereby this procedure can be used by industry and politics for their goals.

5.10 Solar oven

Solar ovens are parabolic mirrors in whose focal point a cooking pot can be variably fixed and heated by solar radiation. Such stoves can replace wood firing. In the Rift Valley in Kenya near Samburu[59], burning fireplaces not only pollutes the environment, but also causes soil erosion due to a lack of offspring from the forest and bushes.

Even though we know that 50% of CO_2 emissions into the atmosphere are caused by industrialized countries, a program for solar ovens can be a win-win situation. On the one hand, it creates jobs in the production of solar ovens (with solar power plants also climate-neutral) and reduces erosion locally.

5.11 Synthetic fuel

Oil, coal and gases have been formed from plants over millions of years in the Earth's history. These take up carbon dioxide and combine it with water and solar energy (photosynthesis) to form solids such as wood, leaves and grass. The resulting fossil fuels are provided with polluted material, which is released during the combustion process and pollutes the environment.[60]

Today's chemistry is so advanced that it can combine carbon dioxide, water and energy in such a way that molecules are formed that cause the least possible environmental damage during the combustion process. Photosynthesis is produced artificially. This synthetic fuel is already on sale at a few filling stations. Sunfire has already successfully launched a pilot project in Germany and is investing in a factory in Norway to use regenerative energy from hydropower plants to produce the synthetic fuel.

The next development step is to extract the carbon dioxide directly from the air. This would create a natural cycle: CO_2 is converted with solar energy / regenerative energy into clean fuel.

Another promising project[61] was concerned with the storage of electrical energy, which is generated in abundance by wind farms in northern Germany and cannot be released to the south. This is an apparatus in which air is stored as compressed air. This then drives a generator if required. Salzgitter has cancelled its participation in the large-scale pilot project because, according to legal regulations, it also has to pay the EEG levy for stored energy. With monetary democracy, funds would be available to implement a large pilot project and to give politicians time to adapt the laws. Even if such an idea had not been successful, the money would not have been wasted. In today's situation, we need ideas that should be explored and tried out without financial support from corporations or government subventions. The above-mentioned project with compressed air has already been partly supported and tested by government subventions. Such an investigation could be introduced as a prerequisite for monetary democracy before an application is passed on to Parliament via the authority administering the project applications.

5.12 Protective measures against climate change

One consequence of climate change is local heavy rainfall, which leads to flooding and widespread destruction of communities. In order to mitigate the consequences, flood polders are being built by the government. The subsidies are provided from government or federal budgets. Various criteria must be taken into account, such as the level of investment. An affected community in the Harz Mountains has the problem that with the support of the state a sufficient protective measure cannot be realised, the sufficient protective measure cannot be approved by the confederative government because of the criteria. Monetary democracy overcomes these different areas of responsibility. A project should be realised optimally for the population, not exaggerated but effective. Transparency serves this purpose. When financing a rough or detailed planning, the topic is publicly distributed. This makes it known to experts from a wide variety of countries who can submit counterproposals or additions to facilitate better implementation.

There will be protective measures against climate change worldwide. The rise in sea levels affects all coastal regions. Here, building up an exchange of knowledge and additionally providing financing are two essential advantages that are not available in their present form.

5.13 Public transport

Not only since the diesel scandal and the impending driving ban for older diesels is the inner city traffic for cars no longer up to date. Not only the exhaust fumes, the fine dust or the background noise are health-damaging factors. With monetary democracy, the following projects are conceivable.

- Stuttgart wants to supplement local public transport with 3 cable cars.
- The importance of the use of bicycle and e-bike has increased. New traffic routes, which are also called bicycle motorways, have a relieving effect on car traffic.

- In the 50s trams were built in the cities of the Ruhr area, the gauge of which even varies from city to city. Due to the mixed financing of the federal, state and city governments, whereby the city is financially responsible for the operation of the tram, there were no modern control units in Cologne. Here, the cities could join forces and carry out overall planning, the implementation of which would take several years. Individual sections could be given to the population as a project for coordination and financing. Before privatising, those responsible should take a look at the London Underground, with which the operator Metronet had to file for bankruptcy in 2007, and the Underground has the most expensive fares in the world.[62]
- In rural communities that have little or no bus transport to the big city and the population is also without doctors, a wide variety of projects could only be financed in the first place. These include the purchase of small buses, an intelligent technology for on-demand transport, etc.
- A major goal at present is e-mobility. The establishment of charging stations in residential areas could accelerate this. There are patents that can use electricity from street lighting. Or the electrical energy could be taken from laid underground lines.
- Today, an utopian project would be to install local public transport for health spa guests in a small community using autonomous vehicles. This is probably as utopian as a tablet that can be folded together and then becomes a mobile phone - now realised in China.

Experience has shown that public transport companies are largely operating at a loss. I can only advise against privatisation with secret contracts. However, the infrastructure of all transport in cities not only includes the part of public transport, but also the part that the city has to provide for roads and their maintenance (potholes). I am in favour of a study in various cities to determine how high the burden is on roads and public transport per passenger kilometre. With the help of monetary democracy, the construction of the cross-generational infrastructure can be tackled cost-effectively.

5.14 Precarious finances for communities

Saarland will serve as an example. There, community cash advances amount to €2.1 billion, effective from the end of 2018[63]. In the Saarland Pact of December 2018, the county government undertook to take over 1 billion of these and to pay €30 million in debt and interest annually. These debts would then be paid off in 2065, i.e. in 45 years. The communities should also pay off the remaining €1.1 billion in 45 years, receiving € 20 million a year for investments. With just over 50 communities[a], each community receives an average investment of €400,000 per year.

The Saarland Pact was praised, among other things, because the communities, districts and the councils are no longer moving the money to be distributed in different directions. This is called a paradigmatic shift. On the other hand, one hopes for additional funds from the confederative government and expects an economic situation that will go well for the long term and low interest rates.

The planning horizon is 45 years over the next generation. If one considers that the Saarland joined the Federal Republic of Germany in 1957, the period of debt reduction is almost in the same range as the mountain of debt was built up.

The financial shortage is supplemented by the consequences of climate change. In 2018, heavy rainfall caused damage of €2.8 million to

[a] Source Wikipedia

Kleinbittersdorf, for example. Although the community receives €0.58 million from the state as part of the needs allocation, it has to pay the rest itself.[64]

I ask myself whether the existing financing system will make debt reduction possible at all.

Monetary democracy is a new way of financing public investment. For communities with 5000 "eligible voters", the grants with the assumed 10€ amount to more than €600,000, i.e. more than those calculated above. The introduction of monetary democracy must also be examined by the communities.

5.15 Planning of a bypass road

In Germany, the population is actively involved in the planning of bypasses, see e.g. the film at: https://rp.baden-wuerttemberg.de/rpk/Dialog/Seiten/default.aspx

In 2010, more than 10,000 vehicles per day were counted on the Jöhlingen / Baden-Württemberg through road with a forecast for the year 2025 of 21,000 vehicles. More details in the given source[65]. After a longer preliminary planning the local council agreed on 16.04.2012 to the 'variant 6' of the relocation of the bypass road B293. The costs are estimated at €28.5 million to be carried by the confederative government. In the confederative government's requirements planning, the new construction was classified as urgent requirement for the year 2030.

With the help of monetary democracy, this project could be realised more cost-effectively for the confederative government and thus earlier. If funding is provided exclusively through monetary democracy, a possible example calculation would look as follows:

Let's assume that the almost 10,000 inhabitants of Jöhlingen succeed in attracting an average of 20,000 people to the ring road in the neighbouring communities via publications and the social media. With this, the financing period would be less than 12 years with the assumed €10 monthly contributions of the federal government. According to the first traffic census in 2010, it would be 8 years earlier than the current planning by the federal government.

6. Implementation of Monetary Democracy

Monetary democracy consists of different parts, which have to be assessed separately when they are introduced. In financial terms, I differentiate between the participation of the population in the government budget and the additional services provided by the participants. The first part can only be sensibly carried out by counties or a union of counties that can guarantee pension payments in addition to tax revenues.

The generation of additional benefits competes with classical capital investments. Here, the basic philosophy of monetary democracy is the essential part: instead of high returns, a pension capital investment and a concrete selection of sustainable, cross-generational projects. This requires initiatives by NGOs, citizen participation, county parliaments and city councils. In order to be able to achieve this effectively, advertising measures are necessary that highlight the further advantages of monetary democracy and monetary climate policy.

6.1 Implementation in communities and cities

In many communities, cities or administrative districts in Germany there is a backlog demand for the restoration and renovation of schools, roads, etc. These cannot be carried out due to lack of financial means and/or due to mixed financing and conflicts of responsibility between the community and the district. Some communities use public-private partnerships (PPP), a form of financing that involves higher costs than necessary.

Under the coordination of the German Association of Cities and Towns, existing structures could be quickly adapted to open up sources of financing similar to monetary democracy.

The portal Bettervest.com[a] is an internet platform for crowdfunding and crowd lending. In contrast to monetary democracy, no guarantees are given for any investments. The individual projects listed there are advertised worldwide.

The platform 'LeihDeinerStadtGeld'[b] (Lend money to your city) is another platform to realize projects. The chairman of the advisory board of the society, the former finance minister Hans Eichel, says on the website: "The offer of LeihDeinerStadtGeld is unique and will change the community financing considerably. At the same time, it promotes social interaction".

Behind this portal stand also banks, which accompany the appropriate capital flows. These would have to be integrated, whereby the following adjustments are necessary:

- There is a guarantee for the repayment by the communities as pension payments instead of high interest.
- The given funds are paid out only at pension beginning as pensions
- The projects must be carried out transparently.
- The personal data as well as the capitals with the inflation hedge and the interest rate are to be made available to the participants. This could be done by integrated life insurers.
- There must be no competition between communities and cities with different interest promises.

---

[a] https://www.bettervest.com/de/?r=5a2b901ac63f020014548e26&c=triodos
[b] https://www.leihdeinerstadtgeld.de

In order to secure the pension payments, the respective community or the community association can have them insured by an insurance company as a precautionary measure.

If, in further steps, a country or Europe introduces parts or the entire monetary democratic structure, the funds and data of the participants who obtain a pension entitlement from it can be passed on to the higher structure.

It becomes clear that the basic building blocks of direct democracy can be laid without legislative changes. There is a lack of initiative on the part of local authorities and cities to agree and implement concerted action.

6.2 Business model for life insurance

The life insurance companies are explicitly listed in the infrastructure of monetary democracy as points of contact for depositors / private individuals. It is now possible to offer life insurance that offers low interest rates and protection against inflation, as provided for by monetary democracy. The insurance representatives can now approach the communities, cities etc. as investors and take up sustainable infrastructure projects. With an advertising campaign by life insurers combined with local advertising by cities, regions, etc., private investors can be found. These conclude a life insurance policy with the allocation of their capital to a concrete project. If this is financed, the payment amount goes directly to the community / regions and the project can be realised.

For the administration of the funds and the personal data a life insurance receives a contribution, which contains the costs and a win margin. If a pension case now occurs, i.e. pension payments become due, then the borrowers, i.e. cities, communities etc., transfer the amounts including the interest and the inflation compensation to the life insurers. The life insurances are only liable if a borrower becomes insolvent. The life insurer receives a premium for this default risk. However, the risk for life insurance policies with public borrowers is extremely low.

If monetary democracy is then introduced at country level or at European level, it must already be established in the treaties that the liability for pension payments is transferred to the country or to the pension fund of monetary democracy and that the risk of a loss of insurance company's assets is thus eliminated.

Life insurers today have the problem of investing the capital of existing contracts profitably. Politicians are therefore being urged to finance public infrastructure through the public-private partnership (PPP) model. However, this model is highly controversial in politics and among the population. In order to escape the dilemma of high returns on life insurance policies, policyholders can be offered a contractual amendment to existing contracts. Insurers can use the model of monetary democracy to revive the negative image of life insurance that has been developing for some time. The following points could have a supporting effect:

- It is not the large asset managers who are confronted with the government in order to invest their money profitably.
- Repayments do not begin until individual investors become entitled to a pension
- The investor decides for himself which project his capital can flow into: infrastructure, environmental or climate projects.

The introduction of such life insurance policies only makes sense if the relevant legal aspects are clear to everyone. I see great opportunities for life insurers to convert their burdensome old contracts into a new legal form and to free themselves from the pressure for high returns.

6.3 Implementation in a country

As mentioned in Chapter 3.1 on the pension fund, some countries already manage a sovereign wealth fund or pension fund.

These funds could be extended to include a part where participants can make project-related contributions as additional benefits. A political, parliamentary decision could introduce the principles of monetary democracy by law (low interest rates / inflation protection / pension payments) from a certain point in time and an existing infrastructure for the presentation of the financing projects.

If the basic principles of monetary democracy are already in place in municipalities or cities, it is necessary to agree on the level of interest and the underlying tables to calculate a pension.

The participation of the population through the national budget is more complex. In the European Union there are different forms of democracy, so that in each country it must be examined how the introduction can take place legally.

In Germany, plebiscitary votes are only possible at country level with different forms, e.g. quorums (minimum electoral participation). The question is to be examined legally whether the participation of the population in the national budget falls under the aspect of plebiscitary co-determination or not. On 13.07.2017, Article 90 of the Basic Law was amended in such a way that Public Private Partnerships (PPPs) become possible as a source of financing for the maintenance and new construction of federal motorways[a]. If an amendment to the Basic Law is necessary for monetary democracy, a majority must be sought. In the other case, the state's payments to the population can be seen as a subsidy for a funded pension.

[a] Federal Law Gazette dated 19.07.2017

In each country the possible legal restrictions must be examined and possible adjustments in the respective constitutions must be sought.

6.4 Implementation in Europe

The European subvention and promotion policy is often criticised. For this I refer to chapter 4.10. The responsible political bodies in Europe, i.e. the European Parliament, the Commission and the European Council, can change the strongly criticised European subvention policy in the sense of monetary democracy. The first step has been taken with a decision to set up the necessary IT infrastructure. Existing computing centres, such as the EIB (European Investment Bank), which manages the EFSI fund, could be integrated. The €270 billion currently not called up could flow into the pension fund. This would already fund a large number of projects. Projects that lack the funds for detailed planning could also be included.

Until the computer platform and the structure of monetary democracy with data exchange between life insurance companies and banks for personal data are established, the current EIB administration could select the projects. However, the criteria would then be based on those of monetary democracy, so that the project applications and descriptions would be published. In order to minimise the influence of elected politicians and the affected governments, a complete introduction of monetary democracy with the rational decision of the population is necessary.

The existing structures of the EU require unanimity in some areas. There is a possibility that individual governments may fear disadvantages in introducing monetary democracy. In this case, a community of 'willing' countries would make sense. Since monetary democracy is essentially based on the decision-making authority of the people, the European Parliament should be able to decide on its rights (prohibition of a project, control possibilities of the realisation of a project, etc.) by majority vote.

This shift of power to the European Parliament corresponds to the will of the people concerned, according to current and audible opinions.

7. Climate policy

7.1 My thesis on climate policy

Among other things, the World Climate Report in October 2018[66] calls for the following:

"If we want to prevent the worst from happening, the 1.5°C limit must be met, but this requires immediate changes in all areas of society. He continues: "It is possible to slow global warming thanks to alternative economic models, different consumer behaviour, but above all governments must take responsibility.

The following picture may emerge for the 'average consumer': As a citizen, I cannot do anything, a new economic model has to emerge that negatively influences my current quality of life and restricts my consumption. It is not me who is responsible, but the government.

In Germany, the energy system transformation is financed by the EEG levy on electricity consumption (excluding major industries), on the eco-tax on fuels and on network charges. These are costs that the minority person has to bear. In France, in November / December 2018, the Macron government wanted to go the same way with eco-taxes on fuels. This was the trigger that the 'yellow vests' took to the streets and caused considerable damage in Paris and elsewhere by violent demonstrators.

The sensible exit from nuclear energy in Germany will necessarily lead to an increased expansion of renewable energies. Wind farms are being built in the north of Germany, which have brought unprecedented growth to the local population[67]. At the same time, the electrical energy generated there cannot be sufficiently transported to the areas to the south because the grids have not yet been expanded. The original plans, which envisaged power lines as overhead lines, were sensibly prevented by many affected citizens through protests. With additional costs of billions, underground lines are now being laid which will not be completed for a few years.

In addition to the CO_2 and methane emissions, which have a major impact on the earth's greenhouse effect, German citizens are also experiencing environmental pollution in other areas. Following the diesel scandal, particulate matter and NOx pollution have entered the debate area.

Let's compare the driving bans in cities for older diesel vehicles with the environmental reports of the corporations that are obliged to be published in Germany. Sabine Braun, sustainability consultant, speaks[68]: "It is true that of course we try not to make things look so bad. There are also alternative methods in cement production that save 80 % of material (using carbon instead of steel). Climate protector Femke de Jong of Karbon Market Watch says: "According to our research, the cement industry is preventing an active change in construction standards, which they see as a threat to their business model. The reporter sums it up as follows: "It is the increasing simulation of climate protection, as if Germany were a single giant VW plant in which environmental standards are often only observed on paper.

As early as summer 2013, a school newspaper[69] will publish a study on the CO_2 pollution caused by airplanes. On average, 380 grams of CO_2 are emitted per person and per kilometre in short-haul traffic. This is more than twice as much as the average consumption of a car. On long-distance flights, such as the Airbus A380, 86 grams of CO_2 are emitted per passenger per kilometre. As an example: if three girlfriends fly from Stuttgart to Milan, the atmosphere is polluted with 448 kg CO_2 for the 390 km flight. A family with 2 children who go on holiday by car would thus travel 2,890 kilometres.

Prof. Stefan Gössling, an expert on climate policy, speaks on this subject today[70]: "I don't know of any other human activity that produces as many emissions in such a short time as flying. There is certainly less inefficient air traffic within Germany and for this reason it should be abolished". Mr Gössling says: "There is only one thing that helps: less flying! The renunciation of a family participating in the long-term project of the Institute for Climate Impact Research has saved the largest amount of CO_2 emissions of 6 tonnes when they renounced a holiday flight[a]. And the pupils say: "People make things simply without knowing what will become of it!

Citizens are well aware that 50 % of climate change is caused by CO_2 emissions from industrialised nations. They also know, however, that the industrial nation USA withdrew from the Paris climate agreement under Trump and that oil is extracted from shale sand in America and Canada in an environmentally damaging way. They also know that China generates the bulk of its electricity from coal-fired power plants and that new coal-fired power plants are planned in developing countries such as Bangladesh. They also know that the only agreement reached at the climate conference in Paris in 2015 was that the earth should not warm up to more than 2°C, or better 1.5°C. In December 2018 in Katowice it was first agreed on a set of rules on how CO_2 emissions in a country should be determined and that the results of the Intergovernmental Panel on Climate Change should be recognised. Citizens can draw the well-founded conclusion from the failure of international politics and the ineffective procedures in Germany, combined with the high costs for ordinary citizens that their own actions do not bring about any significant progress in climate policy.

And there are enough organisations that simply deny climate change[b]. In America there is the arch-conservative 'The Heartland Institute', whose member Jay Lehr boasts that he has successfully pushed the Trump administration to abandon the Paris climate agreement. In the European

[a] Mittagsmagazin ARD/ZDF (3.12.2018)

[b] Monitor dated 08.12.2018, Tagesschau 24

Parliament climate denier Steward Agnew, rapporteur for the Committee on Agriculture and Rural Development, has come to the conclusion that there is no problem for the Commission to solve due to the lack of climate change (the report was rejected by the majority of the committee). In Germany, Mr Karsten Hilse of the AFD spoke of the 'false doctrine of man-made climate change'. Behind this are arch-conservative think factories, such as the European Institute for Climate and Energy (EIKE), which have succeeded in having the climate denier, Prof. Nir Shaviv, of the Hebrew University of Jerusalem RACAH, Institute of Physics, allowed to present these scientifically refuted theses in the Bundestag without contradiction.

Who can accuse the 16% of Germans of believing that there is no climate change?[a]

If you look for political parties in Germany that take climate change seriously and want to bring about change, you cannot ignore the Bündnis 90/Die Grünen party. Annalena Baerbock, head of the party, said in a summer interview on ZDF on 05.08.2018: "Climate policy only works if you are in power". Ms Baerbock is chairman of the party that wanted to introduce Veggie Day, which has been withdrawn. In an interview at the climate conference in Katowice in 2018, the Federal Minister for the Environment announced that, if voluntary restrictions are not effective, legislation would have to be resorted to.

In canteens, it has been established that when the CO_2 emissions of different dishes are stated, customers take these figures seriously and increasingly choose dishes with low CO_2 emissions. The introduction of such a label in supermarkets reminds me of the 'traffic light', which is intended to highlight significantly the negative components of foods such as sugar and salt for the end consumer. To the best of my knowledge, this regulation was prevented by the German government. In Katowice it was reported that when switching from beef to pork, methane emissions

[a] Monitor dated 08.12.2018, Tagesschau 24

from cattle can significantly reduce greenhouse gases. If one pursues this goal, in the Swabian sketch series 'Hannes und der Bürgermeister' (Hannes and the Mayor) the popular roast beef in oxen must be renounced. How could legislation be implemented nationally and internationally?

Let's summarise briefly: Citizens are confronted with higher costs of living in the fight against climate change and experience how Americans can continue without restrictions. Politicians do not achieve self-imposed goals and 'threaten' with restrictive laws. Growth figures in the automobile industry and in the number of passengers in air traffic are celebrated by politicians and the stock exchange, but at the expense of the environment. International traffic produces vast amounts of papers and reports that are no longer comprehensible to the average consumer - and demand democratic patience. Neither politicians nor scientists have succeeded in convincing citizens of climate policy. They have failed because of this never ending task. There is not only a danger that the climate targets will be missed, but also that the fragile structure of democracy could collapse.

The citizens must be given the opportunity to act, the citizens who want to act positively and change. Monetary democracy and monetary climate policy, taking account of efficiency, are structured in this way. I call on the political and scientific elites to discuss the two complementary models in public, to fix the variables indicated in a meaningful way and to take the first steps towards their introduction.

7.2 State at the moment (unchanged takeover from 2015)

There are over 500 environmental programmes worldwide, some with their own secretaries of government. Since the first environmental conference in Stockholm in 1972, almost 200 multilateral, i.e. equal and cooperative environmental agreements have been reached. The United

Nations Environment Programme (UNEP) is based in Nairobi and is to be reformed.

The G7 summit in Elmau in June 2015 brought the self-commitment of the industrialised countries to bring the carbon dioxide emissions resulting from the burning of fossil fuels to zero at the end of the century (decarbonisation). By 2050, greenhouse gases are to be reduced by 40% to 70% compared with 2010 by the contracting parties to the UNFCCC in accordance with the IPCC recommendations. With regard to fluorocarbons (HFCs), reference was made to the Montreal Protocol.

At the climate conference in December 2015 in Paris (COP21), a "legal agreement ... under the United Nations Framework Convention on Climate Change (UNFCCC)" is to be reached.

In Elmau, the G7 Group decided to continue the scientific and technical exchange of knowledge, the integration of public capital, private financing, laws and regulations in all countries, etc. This is to be promoted by international institutions and agreements.

The following explicit reference is made to private funding: "Financing models with a high mobilisation effect are needed to overcome existing obstacles to investment".

On 03.08.2015 US President Barak Obama published his new environmental goals. The coal-fired power plants are to reduce CO_2 emissions by 30% by 2030 and the use of renewable energies is to be stepped up. It is very difficult to implement these targets in the USA, as the causes of climate change are often denied by mankind and industry fears excessive costs.

On 04.08.2015 the German Federal Environment Agency published the Environmental Report 2015. In all publications and announcements known to us we lack an easily understandable, fair and future-oriented set of rules, which can be used internationally and controlled, but can be implemented individually, i.e. according to national laws, in every country.

7.3 Criticism of the political approach

7.3.1 Causes of climate change are not taken into account

In international agreements, states commit themselves to reducing CO_2 emissions within their own borders. National laws and regulations serve this purpose.

However, consumption in the industrialised countries also causes CO_2 emissions in other countries. One example is the flaring of natural gas when oil is produced by internationally active companies such as Shell, BP, etc. in countries such as Niger, Gabon and Russia. Despite the ban in Europe on flaring the associated gas, oil produced in this way is imported.[71]

In the palm oil business, the rainforest is deforested and replaced by single crop farming. The indigenous population groups are destroyed and their homeland is polluted with millions of litres of pesticides. Four hundred companies in the palm oil business work together in an organisation with the WWF, which certifies the sustainability of the management. Greenpeace describes the WWF's certification system as a fraudulent labelling system.[72] Protecting the rainforests as the 'green lungs of the earth' is a task for the entire human race.

Although the causes of climate change are also to be found in the industrialised countries, there is no set of rules that takes into account the efforts of these countries in another country as a contribution to climate protection.

7.3.2 Involvement of private investors

As emphasized in Elmau 2015, 'financing models with a high mobilisation effect' are to be created. This is actively pursued by politicians. In July 2015, for example, the Federal Ministry of Economics and Energy invited participants to an information event on financing in Latin American countries[73]. As described in the Monetary Democracy, however, private capital does not work across generations, but profitably on an investment horizon.

There is no international set of rules that reward cross-generational investments in terms of environmental and climate protection.

7.3.3 Climate change and national sovereignty

It is true that world climate conferences bring the problem of climate change closer to all governments. Behind this lies the much-loved obviousness of the sovereignty of countries, as adopted by the UN. At these conferences one tries to come by 'democratic argument' to sets of rules which are accepted by all. Each country defines self-obligatory targets. A change of government, as in Germany or the USA, changes the policy, abandons ambitious targets or even withdraws from the climate agreement.

If one compares the threat of climate change with an attack by 'Martians' threatening humanity, it becomes clear that the nationalistic behaviour of countries like the USA, Russia and China is not up to the problems. Only when one sees an army of Martians, these countries would work together. This is not the case with climate change. In every country, however, there are people, mostly minorities, who want to do something about climate change and local pollution.

There is no internationally effective system that is independent of governments and that can (allow) actually implemented climate change projects with money on a permanent basis (including minorities).

7.3.4 International control committees and measurement methods

In the negotiations to date and the proposals for the Paris Conference, there are only declarations of intent by individual countries to reduce emissions of climate-damaging substances. Every country with the most diverse economic systems, rules and support options must find its own ways of implementing the targets.

There is no approach that rewards financial, international efforts to protect the environment. There is no international platform where simple measuring methods can be further developed and standardised. There is no marketplace where the supply of technical solutions and financial resources is compared to an enquiry.

7.3.5 Distinction between climate and environmental protection

Coal-fired power plants emit not only the climate-damaging CO_2, but also toxic substances such as mercury or soot particles. Smog locally pollutes the air and polluted rivers testify to environmentally harmful production methods.

Climate agreements neglect and trivialise visible (and local) environmental pollution. For this reason, the possibility is avoided that sceptics of climate change could more easily agree to international agreements.

7.4 Premises of the monetary climate politic

- Every country has the right to have economic growth and an increase in the standard of living of its population.
- Each country undertakes to budget for environmental protection a certain percentage of its Gross Domestic Product (GDP), the allowance amount (AB) referred to here. This allowance amount consists of investments made by public budgets, private investments and investments made by domestic regions in other countries.
- The investments are not bound to a specific location, but can be made anywhere in accordance with bilateral agreements.
- In the case of an investment sum, the efficiency of the technical innovation is taken into account, see next chapter.
- The result of each investment is published in a technically transparent and uniform manner.

7.5 Monetary valuation on an investment

A concrete investment (IN) is taken into account as an allowance amount (AB) to its voluntary commitment according to Chapter 7.4 as follows:

AB = IN - EKB where EKB is the efficiency - reduction amount

The EKB expresses how effective the technical measure is. It is calculated by multiplying the investment sum by the efficiency W of the technical measure:

EKB = IN * W

That is $W = \frac{UWBneu}{UWBalt}$

UWB_{neu} is the environmental impact per energy unit (kWh or MWh) (e.g. CO_2 emissions, soot particles etc.) after the investment, UWB_{alt} before the investment, or in the case of energy savings the energy demand after and before a modernisation. In general:

$$AB = IN - IN \cdot \frac{UWBneu}{UWBalt} = IN \cdot (1 - \frac{UWBneu}{UWBalt})$$

This type of calculation is illustrated by various examples:

7.5.1 New buildings

(Wind, solar, water (tide, waves, etc.)) and heating equipment (solar collectors, solar ovens, etc.) **without** environmental impact. Here, the UWB_{neu} is zero, so the full investment amount is counted as an environmental measure.

Example: Solar power plants are currently being built in desert countries south of the Mediterranean Sea[74]. The DESERTEC project was already written off after the withdrawal of large corporations such as Siemens or

Bosch, but is being revived by Roland Berger, who is well-known in Germany. Due to the unstable situation in the Middle East caused by the turmoil of war, unfortunately only a few countries are still eligible for this project. A concrete investment or financial support from an industrialized country could, for example, not only create growth in Tunisia, but also pursue an active foreign policy. In the case of mixed financing, e.g. Tunisia and an industrialised country, the allowance amount can be divided.

7.5.2 Modernization

(e.g. installation of filters in coal-fired power plants) or replacement of existing systems (e.g. combined heat and power systems for old heating systems, heat pumps etc.)

If, for example, the UWB_{neu} is still 70% of the old environmental pollution, then follows:

$$AB = IN \cdot (1 - \frac{0{,}7 \cdot UWBalt}{UWBalt}) = 0{,}3 \cdot IN$$

This means that only 30% of the investment sum is credited. For the operator of an installation, the advantage could be that he complies with new limits with a lower investment and thus achieves a longer service life.

If the UWB_{neu} is on the other hand 10% of the UWB_{alt}, i.e. a reduction of the environmental pollution by 90%, then 90% of the investment sum is counted.

This example illustrates the flexibility of the rules and regulations. Even greater room for manoeuvre results if several pollutants are taken into account.

If, for example, the emissions of CO_2 and nitrogen oxide (NOx) remain the same with an investment, but SO2 (sulphur to 2/3), HG (mercury by 90% to 10%) and dust/soot (to 1/3) are reduced, the following picture could emerge with the installation of an SCR catalyst in a lignite-fired power plant:

$$W = \frac{UWB_{neu}}{UWB_{alt}} = \frac{CO_{2neu}}{CO_{2alt}} \cdot \frac{NO_{xneu}}{NO_{xalt}} \cdot \frac{SO_{2neu}}{SO_{2alt}} \cdot \frac{HG_{neu}}{HG_{alt}} \cdot \frac{Staub_{neu}}{Staub_{alt}} = 1 \cdot 1 \cdot \frac{2}{3} \cdot 0{,}1 \cdot \frac{1}{3} = \frac{1}{45}$$

.

For the government's allowance amount, this is the result:

$$AB = IN \cdot (1 - W) = IN \cdot (1 - \frac{1}{45}) \approx 0{,}98 \cdot IN$$

which is about 98% of the total investment.

If one adds the efficiency of energy efficiency, e.g. through a new burner, E_{nach}/E_{vor} as a factor (while at the same time reducing CO_2 emissions), even better values result. A weighting of the pollutants could also be included in the formula. Dust and the more dangerous mercury, for example, can be weighted separately.

7.5.3 Use of ‚energy waste'

This includes the burning off, of natural gas during oil production. Technically feasible is the drive of generators with this gas and the investment is fully chargeable. Source 71 states that in Ecuador the investment of USD 150 million is already amortised in two years through the use of the accompanying gas.

The CO_2 certificates now released will enable Ecuador not to modernise other industries that pollute the environment. However, our concept of a continuous, transparent commitment requires new investments in environmental protection as soon as the percentage of GDP has not yet been reached. We can therefore speak indirectly of an economic stimulus package.

Another possible use of 'energy waste' is the use of heat from (existing) large power plants in district heating systems, the investment sum of which could also be fully recognised.

At the Hannover Fair 2015, new large-scale technical plants were presented which were still rated negatively by the Töpfer Commission on the phase-out of nuclear energy in Germany as 'too low on efficiency'. Firstly, I would like to mention the entry point into hydrogen technology for electricity from wind or solar power plants that is not immediately used. The hydrogen, however, can be safely fed into existing natural gas pipelines up to a certain percentage. On the other hand, a plant uses the superfluous electricity to produce artificial methane, which could be made available to the vehicles as fuel directly via a filling station network.

Both technical innovations mentioned in the last paragraph compete with other systems and infrastructures. During the energy revolution in Germany, much is being done with wind power plants in the north, whereby the electrical energy is to be transported via electricity grids to the industrial south. In addition, during smaller phases of power generation, e.g. when there is no wind, previously generated amounts of energy must be stored in other systems. All technical investments for this general conversion of the electricity supply in Germany are therefore included in the capital charge as the allowance amount (AB).

7.5.4 New coal and gas power plants

If industrialisation and the standard of living in a country increase, this goes hand in hand with a higher environmental impact. In order to enable growth nevertheless and to take environmental pollution into account, these new power plants must be built as environmentally friendly as possible. They are therefore more expensive. The possible approach is as follows:

$$AB = IN \cdot (1 - \frac{UWBneu}{UWBdurch}).$$

UWB_{durch} is the average UWB of the existing power plants in this country per amount of energy generated (MWh).

This ensures that average emissions continue to fall and that the government meets its environmental obligations with economic growth.

7.5.5 Investments in electricity grids

Wind and solar power are weather-dependent and the electrical energy generated from them has to be transported over long distances: in Germany, wind energy from the north to the south, in future (hopefully) solar power from the southern countries (Desertec) to the north. Here bipolar HVDC ground and sea lines could become a legal obligation. These lines are more accepted by the population and are much more environmentally friendly. We do not know whether the currently laid HVDC submarine cable to Norway for the use of reservoirs as electricity storage or the planned underground lines (north-south route) to Bavaria are designed bipolar. The 250 km long Baltic Cable from Lübeck Bay (Germany) to Malmö (Sweden) is not bipolar. As a result, the sea is to be polluted locally with caustic sodium solution and, on the other hand, rust corrosion on sunken poison gas ammunition from the world wars is to be increased[75].

For grid stability in multi-renewable energies such as wind power plants and solar power plants, weather-related energy storage systems are needed that can provide the necessary grid stability. These are new hydroelectric power plants such as those in the Black Forest, battery storage facilities, power plants powered by synthetic fuels or gases, etc. These investments, which are necessary for an energy system transformation, should also be taken into account as an allowance amount.

7.5.6 Energy savings

Here the efficiency W is used by the energy consumption after (E_{nach}) and before (E_{vor}) a measure, i.e.

$$AB = IN \cdot (1 - \frac{Enach}{Evor}).$$

If, for example, 20% energy savings are achieved in the insulation of a house, i.e. 80% is still required, then the following applies:

$$AB = IN \cdot (1 - \frac{Enach}{Evor}) = IN \cdot (1 - \frac{80\% \cdot Evor}{Evor}) = 0{,}2 \cdot IN$$

Therefore 20% of the investment amount will be accounted.

7.5.7 Protection of forests 'green lungs of the earth'

The clearing of huge areas for soya cultivation in Brazil or palm oil production in Borneo is destroying the earth's lungs: plants convert CO2 into oxygen. The ecological footprint of humans prevents the earth from regenerating itself.

The establishment and protection of national parks is the task of the respective county. The one-off and running costs for the establishment and maintenance of a national park are to be fully taken into account as an allowance amount.

7.5.8 Abbreviations in calculation methods

E: Energy consumption or energy use

IN: Investment total in EURO (currency)

AB: Allowance amount for which the government has committed itself

EKB: Efficiency reduction amount. This is the investment amount multiplied by the efficiency of the technical measurements

W: Efficiency that is the environmental impact-new divided by environmental pollution-old

UWB: Environmental impact per energy unit, e.g. MWh

E: Energy consumption or use

alt: Old

neu: New

durch: Average

7.6 Technical transparency

At a conference in Seville in spring 2015, representatives of industry, governments and environmental organisations discussed and agreed on the future limit values for coal-fired power plants. There is the accusation that these limit values were often set by the industry lobby and entire passages of the industry text were copied into the final declaration[76]. Some limit values have been set, which are weaker than the limit values set by China for its new coal-fired power stations. One example is the expensive SCR catalyst, which can drastically reduce NOx emissions but is rejected by industry.

Our approach, on the other hand, can be implemented continuously with continuous measurements and alongside the above system. Coordination and publication could be done centrally by the UN and be controllable.

Following the example of TTIP, a standardisation of the technical standards should be established. Most of these are measurement methods that could be developed by independent institutes and universities.

In the training courses for natural science subjects, standard tests can be carried out by the students. Experiments, such as Millikan's experiment, have been carried out millions of times.

In our concept, a country has to make investments while taking efficiency into account. This obligation can be appropriately transferred to the enterprises by laws, ordinances or subsidies. If the country, e.g. in coal-fired power plants, adds the other environmentally harmful substances (soot, mercury, etc.) for national regulation, one can imagine the wide scope for design that our constant, transparent concept has and which favours technical progress.

7.7 Possibilities of national implementation

7.7.1 Energetic refurbishment of buildings and houses

In Germany, the Renewable Energies Heat Act (EEWärmeG) anticipates the EU directive on renewable energies issued on 23 April 2009.

New buildings are required to use renewable energies (RE). In future, old buildings will also be subject to renovation in accordance with the EU Directive. The law contains financial support options for owners, rules for rent increases, etc. In each case, the market should decide which refurbishment for a building the owner considers sensible.

Every building needs an 'energy permit'. Different methods are mentioned for the calculation: With the consumption certificate the actual costs for the heating of the last years are used and with the demand certificate the building technology is theoretically evaluated with type and thickness of the walls, size of the windows etc. as basis. The energy certificate is only intended to enable a rough comparison of buildings. On the basis of the energy permit, suggestions for energetic renovation can be accepted.

In the case of thermal insulation with polystyrene-like panels, the percentages of possible energy savings were not correct. This type of insulation is promoted by advertising and very often used in private houses. It is prohibited in public buildings because of the risk of fire. In Germany, the material was classified as flame-retardant, contrary to the European classification, where it is classified as flammable. Furthermore, the insulating properties are tested by the FIW Institute in Munich during the production of the panels. The FIW (Forschungsinstitut für Wärmeschutz in München e.V.) is also financed by manufacturing companies, so that it is assumed that the industry controls itself.

In a measurement by independent institutes, approx. 40% of the panels delivered did not meet the specified requirements. Also the promised heat savings are a large controversy topic. The Fraunhofer Institut for building engineering made two scientific investigations in the 80's and came to the result that the values measured in practice do not reach the theoretically before calculated insulation values. In particular, thermal bridges are said to have occurred at the corners of buildings. The insulation boards must be renewed usually after approximately 20 years. Nevertheless, this type of house insulation has become politically accepted in Germany and is promoted. Afterwards the plates are special waste[77 78].

In Germany an effective error culture and/or the aftercare philosophy is missing. Our approach requires a subsequent measurement regarding the energy saving or a measurement of the actual energy demand, internationally and standardised. Transparency in monetary democracy will ensure that techniques with little efficiency are used less frequently.

7.7.2 The dilemma of today's legal regulations

Coal-fired power plants have very high CO_2 emissions and other pollutants. Following a change in the law, these emissions were to be reduced, whereas Vattenfall initiated arbitration proceedings against the Federal Republic of Germany for the Hamburg power plant. It was agreed that the limit values would be lowered in Germany. Thus Germany saved itself a large compensation payment, whereby the air is further polluted.

In our approach, there are two obligations for Germany: towards the power plant owner and the monetary voluntary commitment as an allowance amount.

With the help of monetary democracy and climate policy, other possibilities for an agreement would have become probable. In particular, that filters or catalytic converters could be installed in the Hamburg power plant.

7.7.3 Example of bilateral cooperation

In Chapter 7.5.2 it was explained that the capital charge for modernisation can amount to almost 100% of the investment sum. If there are companies in the industrial country Germany that can carry out a technical modernisation, one can imagine the following situation: If a poor country like Romania reduces the permissible limits for power plants, a situation can arise in which the power plant operators cannot finance a conversion. On the other hand, Germany, for example, would like to meet its monetary self-commitment and is looking for effective investment opportunities. If most of the modernisation measures are financed from Germany via the pension fund of monetary democracy, the following situation arises: Germany can meet its self-commitment to the offset amount with lower costs and greater efficiency. The power plant operator receives a cost-effective refurbishment of the plant and meets the new limits. German industry has used the technology to promote exports.

And, last but not least, the environment is less polluted. Thus, a general win-win situation arose.

7.8 Implementation of the UNO

The United Nations (UN) has different suborganisations that deal with global tasks: UNICEF the Children's Rights, WHO the World Health Organisation, etc.

There are several developments that threaten the earth to such an extent that the existence of humanity is endangered: climate change, overpopulation, nuclear armament, conventional armament resulting in local warfare, environmental pollution.

The International Atomic Energy Agency (IAEA) was founded to combat the nuclear threat and reports regularly to the UN Security Council. This agency has the possibility of monitoring compliance with the rules in countries after its approval.

There are currently more than 500 multilateral environmental organisations, many of which have their own secretaries of government and no links between them. The United Nations Environment Programme (UNEP) is based in Nairobi, Kenya, and is to be reformed to bring these agreements under one roof. The issue of the environment should be placed on the same level as peace, security, the economy, health and trade (as of 2015 - source Wikipedia).

We demand such a suborganisation of the UNO. It can build a marketplace in which the supply of technical solutions and financial means can be compared to an enquiry. Such a platform, easily understandable in different languages, makes it much easier to bring together different countries in a common fight against climate change.

7.9 Summary of climate policy

The concept of monetary climate policy, taking efficiency into account, is a pragmatic complement to the targets set by individual countries in climate conferences. In connection with monetary democracy, not only financial resources are generated, but we also abandon profit-oriented thinking and enter into generation-overlapping, global and responsible action.

- The concept provides answers to these questions:
- How much money does a country invest in environmental policy?
- How efficiently are the funds invested?
- Which technologies should be used sensibly in the long term?
- How are demand and supply (monetary and technical) brought together?

Future environmental agreements will be simpler and more transparent to achieve with an agreement on the level of the monetary commitment and the international controlling system anchored in the concept.

8. Renunciation of much-loved obviousness

What is the use of the term '*much-loved obviousness*'? In psychology, one also speaks of belief. Such beliefs are a premise for people to be able to move in their environment and to establish appropriate contact with their fellow human beings. It corresponds to a dogma with the following definition[a]: "By a dogma one understands a fixed definition or a fundamental, normative doctrinal statement, whose claim to truth is established as irrevocable".

As an example, I mention the time as it is presented in Chapter 1. We humans cannot perceive that time is different in other places. First the theory, then the verification by experimental measurements led to the fact that ever more humans with this strange characteristic of the time befriended and/or accepted.

Here I use the term '*much-loved obviousness*', as some examples in the following are no longer self-evident for many people.

8.1 Darwin's theory of evolution

Prof. Dr. Joachim Bauer, brain researcher and physician at the University Hospital of Freiburg, commented[79]: "...since Charles Darwin recognised the fact of evolution,... the opinion has prevailed that egoism is the absolutely predominant principle in biology. This is where ... a decisive change has taken place since about 15 years. More and more biologists

[a] See Wikipedia

are recognising that cooperative mechanisms play a central role in biology, that they are at the beginning of life and that without cooperation we would have no development at all in evolution".

The principle of egoism, that the stronger simply wins, seems to represent a personal experience in every individual life. Prof. Dr. Karl-Heinz Brodbeck, philosopher, economist and business ethicist, says correspondingly[80]: "The education of egoists has, one can say, the last 200 years, resulted in the influence of the economy, the rivalry and the competition.

When people come together to form a group, as happened about 10,000 years ago with agriculture and life in cities, quote: "Under these complicated circumstances, when people of different ethnic and linguistic backgrounds lived in the same place, cooperation was more difficult because our tendency to do so was originally limited to the in-group. Typically, people do not trust out-group members to the same extent. Today, conflicts, wars and the like take place between divided ethnic groups that seek their causes of conflict far in the past[81]."

An ancient political means for inner peace is to seek an external enemy to have peace within. Quote[82]: For the sake of fun, I have often claimed that an invasion of the Martians would bring our world together. If the Martians would march towards us, we would pull together."

The sentence derived from Darwin's theory of evolution 'The stronger one wins' is therefore wrong.

Let me illustrate this with Europe as an example. Italy and Germany were fragmented into individual counties and kingdoms. Garibaldi in Italy, Bismarck with the war of 1870/71 united the territories. After the Second World War, Charles de Gaulle and Konrad Adenauer ended the 'hereditary enmity' between France and Germany. The European Economic Community began with the Coal and Steel Community. With the ERASMUS programme and open borders, we now have a unique freedom of movement in Europe.

The political 'block thinking', the expansion of the 'Chinese model' and the diverging European Union, however, bear witness today to the fact that the idea of freedom and prosperity is in danger in Western democracies. President Macron's statement in his speech on the 100th anniversary of the end of the First World War that one acts against one's own values by placing the nation country above the cooperative has not led to any change in the consciousness of the responsible politicians.

Climate change (partly caused by humans) could, like an 'invasion of Martians on earth', bring about a rethinking. Monetary democracy is a system supplement to hold Europe together and offer the world a generation-spanning cooperative ethic for action.

8.2 The sovereignty of the countries are invulnerable

The Charter of the United Nations enshrines the principle of equal rights and self-determination of peoples[a]: all peoples have the right "to determine freely and without outside interference their political status and to pursue their economic, social and cultural development ...". This fundamental right of the peoples has been and is regularly violated. For example the war of aggression in 1939 under Hitler. In the 1950s Mohammad Mossadegh was overthrown with the help of the CIA in Operation Ajax, which today serves as a model for the interventions of other countries through secret services. The term 'banana republic' testifies to the single-crop farming in which large corporations rule and exploit a country. In the 1980s, American President Ronald Reagan attempted to overthrow the Sandinistas in the banana republic of Nicaragua. The USA was sentenced by the International Court of Justice in The Hague to USD 2.4 billion after a lawsuit, which has not yet been paid. The conflict between Russia and Ukraine has been going on for years. The Chinese urge to expand is not only a result of investments. In Australia, politicians were bribed who had to give up their parliamentary work after the revelation.

[a] 48th session 85 Plenary session of 20.12.1993

Another important influence is development policy, which is often associated with local corruption, as is lamented in Germany. The globalised economy has a formative influence on the domestic affairs of other governments.

With monetary democracy, a project can be financed and implemented in any country. The people responsible for the project are known locally and by name. The local government still has the possibility to prevent a project, but does not need financial means to realise it.

8.3 Homo Oeconomicus

Adam Smith's thesis in his economic theory in the 19th century that man acts economically to his advantage turned out to be wrong in the 1980s. Man acts according to feeling, needs reliability and punishes unreliable persons and rules. He acts in alternation between egoistic and old-ruistic motives. The supreme principle, as it can be formulated, is reputation, i.e. standing as a 'good boy'[83].

The further development of economics has been based on this knowledge. Nevertheless the primary task in economics remains how the economy must act in order to generate satisfactory results and growth. The human being becomes the object of the economy instead of seeing that the economy serves the human being.

Monetary democracy goes exactly the opposite way: The people or the ethnic groups determine, without profit maximisation, what the economy has to realize for the general public.

8.4 Triple-down effect

The triple-down effect means that the consumption of rich people through job creation and tax payments also benefits the general public.

This postulate has proved to be wrong. Prof. Dr. Karl-Heinz Brodbeck, philosopher, economist and economic ethicist, says[84]:"... this idea that wealth is slowly trickling through from top to bottom... this idea and hope that economists announced 30 years ago has proved to be a perfect illusion. It did not happen that way, it happened exactly the opposite. Wealth moves from bottom to top and accumulates at the top."

Often people argue against the fact that higher earners not only pay higher taxes and social security contributions, but also higher percentages, thus supporting the weaker. Unfortunately, the middle class in Germany has to bear a tax burden that is about 1% higher than that of the rich[85].

It is obvious that the widening gap between the rich and the poor is a burden and a threat to society. Monetary democracy can only marginally influence the current financial capitalism. If, however, it is successful in the long run, then a change of mind can take place in dealing with saved money, which could limit the effects of financial capitalism. By increasing investments in sustainably producing companies, the real economy can once again be there for people and not the other way round.

8.5 Climate change is not human-influenced

If you park your car in the sun and come back after an hour, the interior is unbearably hot. How is that possible? Well, the sun's rays warm the seats and armartures that heat the interior air. Since the windows are closed, the heated air cannot escape. Even in winter you can observe that the ice on the windows melts first, while the bonnet remains covered with ice - despite the same amount of sunlight.

Now you can imagine the earth like the interior of a car. The air will not be able to disappear into space due to gravity. Now you say that heat radiation into space brings the cooling of the earth, as it has done for thousands of years. And the Earth has had many different climatic periods, ice ages and warm periods. Solar activity is stronger at the moment, so it is getting warmer all the time.

You have warmth in your house and, to save money, you insulate your house. This can be done, for example, with thick walls or thermal insulation panels on the house wall. This insulation prevents less heat from escaping. And a very good insulator is the air, as you can see from the insulating glass panes of your windows. And certain gases, such as methane and carbon dioxide, do not allow heat radiation to pass through at all. They reflect the heat radiation like a mirror reflects the light.

And this is exactly what happens to the earth. We humans slowly and steadily build a mirror for heat radiation by emitting methane and carbon dioxide in the atmosphere. The air is getting warmer and warmer, and this is called the greenhouse effect.

In Germany, 16% of the population deny that climate change exists (at least influenced by people) (see chapter 7.1) and that we could prevent it.

This *much-loved obviousness* that climate deniers have become fond of can have various causes. One of them, compared to the absolute time, is to be seen in the fact that climate change is not perceived by many because it only takes place slowly and steadily. The earth is also so large that the few things we humans bring into the atmosphere do not matter at all. And if it gets two degrees warmer, what difference does it make? The organisation 'Club of Rome', founded in 1968, published the first effects of human action in 1972 with the book 'Limits to Growth'. Slowly the climate change entered the consciousness of the people.

Local pollution caused by car exhaust fumes, such as NOX which bans older diesel engines in German cities, already existed in Los Angeles in the 1940s[86]. The oil industry founded the 'Smoke and Fumer Committee', with chairman Vance N. Jenkins formulating: "The worst thing that can happen to us is that a law is hastily passed to control air pollution". Then came the results of studies commissioned by the oil industry. The

Brannon Report (1957) and the Robinson Report (1968) attributed the increase in climate-damaging gases in the atmosphere to car traffic: "If CO2 values continue to rise, there will be significant increases in temperature. The oil industry published only those parts that raised doubts about global warming and developed a clever PR strategy. Sebastian Schwark, consultant for political communication, describes this as follows: "One links pseudo-science with PR work and forms 'narratives'[a], which all have their claim to truth. The consequence now is that the 'normal person' picks out the narrative as true, which agrees with his *much-loved obviousness*. He has to find his way in life.

In the documentation 'Flared'[87] from the year 2011 the environmental pollution is described, which is produced by the gas burned off with crude oil production. You probably know the pictures of oil fields with the burning flares of the natural gas. The emission of burnt fossil fuels in Europe produces as many exhaust gases as the burning off during oil production in Nigeria. The World Bank is quoted in the documentary in such a way that "at the end of the day, the oil companies profit from the oil and not from the flared gas. We cannot expect corporations and markets to voluntarily forgo their high profits and accept financial losses just because it is good for the environment. So, if the IMF said something like that eight years ago and the American President is shaping his policy like that today, then it must be true!

And now look at the fireplaces of the houses in winter, when the heaters are on, or at the traffic jams on the motorways in the evening traffic or at the beginning of the holidays: the mirror for the heat radiation in the atmosphere is slowly and irretrievably built up by us humans.

If you are a skier, you are well aware of the different nature of the snow at zero degrees and plus 2 degrees. The permafrost in Siberia stores enormous amounts of carbon dioxide. At plus degrees it thaws and the

[a] Wikipedia: Narratives are meaningful narratives that influence the way the environment is perceived.

gas escapes - a 'domino effect'. And that only because water only freezes by chance at temperatures below zero degrees Celsius.

But two degrees of warming, that doesn't make much difference, is now being used as a counterargument. Well, the sea level is rising, then you just have to help the people in the affected areas. And the new agricultural plants that can tolerate the warmer climate can be cultivated or genetically modified to such an extent that we will not starve to death. Are you so sure that we can do that?

And now for the weather. There have always been local heavy rains and periods of heat or cold. That's normal. Let's take a look at the energy needed to increase the earth's atmosphere by two degrees. Like heating the interior of a car, the energy comes from the sun. How long should a candle burn in a car if it is cool outside at night and you want it to be warm in the car? We have transferred this question to the earth's atmosphere. The colleague Dr. Weber and I made rough calculations with two different methods (heat capacity of the air, general gas equation) and came to the same result: In order to warm up the earth's atmosphere by two degrees, humans would have to detonate an atomic bomb of the strength of Hiroshima every second for over two years. This amount of energy is in the heated atmosphere! And this amount of energy influences the daily weather, because it is simply released by heavy rainfall with the consequences of flooding or heat waves. The word of the Year 2018: Hot Seasons.

Are you now convinced of climate change? No? Just as well! I know that such beliefs sit deep inside a person and can only be changed through one's own work with oneself. This is a long and difficult process.

And on the other hand: why do I have to pay for it with the expensive electricity and eco-taxes on petrol and diesel? The wind power operators and the roofs with solar systems - everything I have to pay, is like the minority person. Everything becomes more expensive and at the end of the month I have no more money. And I work in a coal-mining area, lose my job, my existence. It doesn't work that way!

That's right! The majorities of politicians are convinced of climate change and follow the statements of the scientists that we can meet it effectively. That is why we want to make it socially acceptable. In our economically and politically existing system this is only possible with taxes, subsidies and laws. In France this was the reason for the protests of the 'yellow vests'.

Another and better possibility is the monetary democracy presented here. It also supports infrastructure measures that are necessary for structural changes in coal-mining regions. You, as a sceptic of man-made climate change, can speak up for it with your own voice.

And, of course, international organisations such as the IMF must accept that climate change is a reality and build their policies accordingly. A statement, as quoted above in the document 'Flared', is a disdain for those who think of it that can be taken as an insult.

8.6 Money is necessary to provide for the old-age pension

The financial crisis of 2008 led to much insolvency of US banks. Systemically important banks were supported with billions of taxpayers' money. Securities for old-age provision lost their value. It was the belief that financial investments with high profit expectations guarantee a secure old-age provision. Already during the big stock market crash on Wall Street in the 1920s, the whole country slipped into poverty and took large parts of the world economy with it.

In the words of Prof. Dr. Heinrich Bauer[88] I formulate the belief behind it: "If you (believe) that money is a necessary entry ticket for market participation, then there are two fundamental human attitudes. One is the hope of getting money as quickly and easily as possible -... and the constant fear of falling out because I don't have a ticket."

This belief is correct in money-based societies. However, it leads to excesses and the belief that high returns on savings ensure one's own retirement. The frequent recommendation

or even obligation, as in Sweden, to invest in funds is of no use in a bear market. And the high returns must be promised to take away the fear of an inflation that eats up the value of money.

Monetary democracy is drawing the line here. Investments are protected against inflation. Especially in old age it is important to have an environment in which one can participate in the market with limited age-related forces. If one leaves the composition of the environment to investors and profit-oriented companies, if one saves in profit-oriented equity funds or life insurance policies, one destroys the basis for one's own life.

With this understanding and the reliability of monetary democracy, this dogma is pushed into the background and has less negative cross-generational effects.

8.7 Politicians are responsible

In my opinion there have always been personalities who have led to the formation of the group thousands of years ago. Among the Indians they were called chiefs, in Europe kings or emperors. Man gave responsibility for the leadership of the group to a chosen one. In China it is the party under a leader. The 'subservient' follows the instructions, be it out of conviction, be it because of the subject matter, be it for his own benefit, be it out of respect for the leadership or be it out of fear of reprisals by a tyrant. Typically, I feel the saying from the Nazi era: 'If Hitler knew that'.

In representative democracy this behaviour and the expectations of the citizens were transferred to the elected representatives. Despite good will, the decisions are tied to the restrictions of the existing political structure. This limited possibility of action is also wanted and necessary in democracies. As can be read in Chapter 4.3, politicians in a democracy are rarely in a position to adequately meet the expectations of citizens.

With the introduction of monetary democracy, politicians are not only relieved but also deprived of power, since many decisions and financial resources are granted to the people. Further developments in democracy, such as the Irish Citizens' Assembly (see Chapter 4.8), could lead to a new self-understanding of citizens - with fewer expectations and blame on politicians.

8.8 How I live is 'normal'

Let's ask ourselves the question: What is 'normal'?

I quote Prof. Dr. Christoph Wulf, educationalist and anthropologist, Free University Berlin[89]: "Social norms and values shape us from an early age. So we internalise early on exactly how we have to behave .... Not everyone is personally known to us. We must be able to rely on the fact that all members of society will follow the same social values and norms in order to facilitate smooth coexistence. Conformity is the core characteristic of a cultural group."

So normal is how others behave in my group. Individual behaviour is thus determined by the group to which we belong. Workers behave differently than managers, bankers differently than hooligans. And, of course, there is more trust and reliability in people in the 'ingroup' than in people in the 'outgroup'.

If we look at the most diverse cultures and languages in the world, everyone can justifiably claim to live 'normally'. For a development that could stop climate change, all people must be allowed to act 'normally' with this target in mind.

If we also consider the development of democratic structures, I quote Prof. Dr. Rainer Mausfeld[90] on the theses of Walter Lippmann and John

Dewey: "... that both could not have understood each other at all... because they started from almost diametrically opposed images of man and because they pursued almost diametrically opposed political political targets...". Lippmann was concerned with the question of how power can be organised efficiently in a modern industrial society. Dewey was concerned entirely with the tradition of the enlightenment, "...how can power be effectively contained". To put it in a shorter form, Lippmann's position has prevailed in America with the development of neoliberalism.

Dewey quotes: "As long as secrecy, partiality, prejudice, misrepresentation, propaganda and sheer ignorance prevail in informing the public, there is no way to judge the political intelligence of the masses. The same source refers to studies by psychologist Philip Tetlock, who examined predictions by experts on complex decisions of social issues with those of the ordinary population. Quote: "Experts are, what a surprise, just people. They show the same cognitive errors like normal citizens. But there is one special feature that strikes him. Experts show more sophisticated justifications for false predictions, that they actually somehow would have been quite right after all."

If we look at the cultural differences in the world in different regions, there are historically many other views about the human image. These views determine political structures. Because of conformity as the main characteristic of a cultural group, each individual acts 'normally'. Since the reliability and trust in the the 'in-group' persons are higher, a new 'normality' of action is necessary as a premise for the fight against climate change.

With monetary democracy, through the international financing of concrete projects, a system is created in which every participant can regard every fellow human being as an 'in-group human being'. For the first time there is a system with which every human being can act concretely. Thus, the newer findings about human evolution can be implemented, contrary to Darwin's theory of evolution. The use of this system is then regarded as 'normal action' if it can be used in society from 'childhood', as suggested in Chapter 4.14.

8.9 The free market regulates everything

I quote Christian Felber, freelance publicist, Vienna[91] : "The father of modern economics, the Scottish economist Adam Smith, assumed in the 18th century that an invisible hand would tame egoisms. The markets would regulate themselves and self-interest and profit would ultimately lead to the prosperity of nations. If everyone takes care of himself, says Adam Smith, then everyone is taken care of, so to speak ... that was the revolutionary discovery. And we don't need morality because competition ensures that the egoists form a barrier to each other."

History has decided otherwise. Manchester capitalism led Karl Marx to write his epochal work 'Capitalism', which led to a world revolution in Russia and the Eastern block. The economic crisis of the 1920s prompted US President Roosevelt to introduce the New Deal. The financial crisis of 2008 also showed that the free market cannot order itself. The fact that Larry Fink of all people, the founder of the asset management company BlackRock, is the main author of the crisis rescue plan for the banks after the American financial crisis in 2008 proves that profiteers of the free market also have to comply with regulations[92]. Today several opponents of regulation are directly at the cabinet table of Donald Trump, such as Jay Clayton (2018), the head of stock exchange supervision, who advised Goldman Sachs, among others.

Ronald Reagan's 1988 quote, ex-president of the United States, when the consequences of climate change first became known, shows just how deeply rooted this dogma is among those responsible[93]: "Our path to prosperity does not lie in bureaucracy or the distribution of goods, but in less national interests and more freedom for the entrepreneur.

It is difficult for me to judge whether this dogma is a principle of faith in the true sense or whether it is enforced in politics with lobbyists out of self-interest. In Germany, the government of the Social Democrats and the Greens has made it possible to liberalise the capital market for hedge funds. This is more likely to strengthen the importance of the financial centre of the Frankfurt Stock Exchange.

The curious results that the free market can assume are illustrated in Chapter 5.4 using the example of Internet expansion in Germany.

Monetary democracy does not restrict the free market. It is a system for financing intergenerational projects. These investments are tasks of the public authorities and cannot be realized with the principles of the free market.

8.10 The government needs major investors

If we look at subvension policies for private investment, they are aimed at industry and SMEs[a]. Among other things, subsidies are there to achieve political, overall development targets.. In November 2018 it became known[b] that the German government is releasing €1 billion to the large scale industry for 2 plants to produce batteries according to the latest technical know-how.

Nevertheless, there are private initiatives without subsidies that can sweep an entire village along with a lot of commitment. One example is the town of Schönau in the Black Forest, which today has made its town practically self-sufficient from a wide variety of renewable energies and is a pioneer and role model for many communities. The initiators were a wedded pair who achieved this through persuasiveness and diligence.

[a] Small and medium-sized enterprises

[b] ARD news

To finance new ideas for start-up companies, trade fairs have developed at which private individuals can be given targeted risk capital. For example, drones have been developed for the transport of medicines and their release for Germany is currently being examined. There are companies that develop autonomous flight taxis, etc. What all these start-up companies have in common is that they have to assert themselves in the market. They have to attract customers in order to sell their products.

The *much-loved obviousness* calling for major investors has to be verified. Not all start-ups' products can establish themselves in the market if they serve a clientele that is in financial need. I am talking here about communities and towns. Chapter 5.13 - Examples - outlines future projects that are perhaps unimaginable today.

NGOs[a] have also established themselves financially, but do not receive any subsidies according to the existing criteria. The much-loved obviousness that NGOs are enemies of capitalism and government must be dropped. Their target is a better world and this corresponds to the goal of monetary democracy. Their international interdependencies offer opportunities to promote climate and environmental projects worldwide, which should be used.

The dogma that capital must come from the 'rich' to build and maintain infrastructure must also be abandoned. With taxes and savings, the people have more than enough resources to finance them themselves and know what is important - they need monetary democracy for this.

8.11 The political centre is democratic

I refer to Prof. Dr. Rainer Mausfeld's remarks on elite democracy and opinion management[94].

[a] Non-governmental organisation

"The triumph of neoliberalism ... led to a transformation of the traditional people's parties, which lost their social roots to the extent that they joined the triumph of the neoliberal revolution. ... The classic popular parties have ... increasingly integrated themselves into the government's apparatus of power for self-preservation ... so that their core has become largely interchangeable."

Party researcher Peter Mair used the term "cartel party" to describe the new type of large parties: "These cartel parties have now declared themselves to be the centre, namely a centre with no alternative ... and at the same time they have declared that the traditional distinction between left and right has become obsolete.

The thinking of neo-liberalism has become a dogma in people's minds, as Gerhard Schröder's quote as Federal Chancellor shows: "There is no left-wing or right-wing economic policy, only good or bad economic policy". And Prof. Mausfeld adds that the motto of Italian fascism was 'left and right have become obsolete'. And continues: ... "the political centre was an extremist position in its contempt for democracy, ... especially in the disempowerment of the legislature by the executive."

In my view on democracy (see Chapter 4.1) another phenomenon comes to bear, which I will explain using the example of the Green Party. The Green movement was born of civil disobedience to the construction of nuclear power plants. The demonstrations were often non-violent and their power was that sit-in blockades can be an effective means of changing political opinion. There were also excesses with violence, whereby the later Foreign Minister Joschka Fischer is said to have been identified as a stone thrower in a photo. The founding of the Green Party was then based on the recognition that political change could only take place within government structures. Civil disobedience can thus reverse individual laws, as the example of the eco-tax in France by the Yellow West shows (effective from early December 2018). Otherwise the political structure of a government will remain sluggish and non-movable. A discourse on the further development of democratic structures only takes place in exceptional cases, as the Citizens' Assembly in Ireland or the citizen participation in Filderstadt shows. However, the power structures remain intact.

Prof. Mausfeld goes on: "... this ideology of the alternative solitude naturally implies that the public room for debate is limited to what the centre declares to be the centre. The elimination of the categories left and right (more precisely the term left) means that the public room for debate as a premise for democracy is concentrated on the themes of the centre. The set of solutions to social problems is now limited to what is reasonable, and everything that is outside the public room for debate is now described as unreasonable, irrational, extremist and populist today".

As Prof. Mausfeld pointed out, this development has empirically proven that the 'middle without alternatives' itself is shaking democracy. The fine structure of democracy shows a weak point.

The existing structures of a political system that determines the balance of power within the community are hardly capable of reform. A turn to nationalism with the restriction of democratic structures is possible, as is demonstrated in Poland, Turkey and Hungary with populism and privileged, financially strong groups. To make an existing democracy more democratic, people's parties are too strongly integrated into the system - and seek the democratic centre.

The model of monetary democracy emerged through brainstorming in a room for debate outside the dominant political system. It does not attack the existing power structures and can be introduced everywhere regardless of the system. The political decision-makers, be it the government or the parliament, continue to have full control. For Europe, the positive effect is that the historically grown complexity and 'ungovernability' will make a step towards a democracy close to the people.

8.12 People are stupid

The terrible historical experience of National Socialism has led to a correction of the constitution in Germany. The Basic Law expressly states that the parties participate in the formulation of political will (Article 21) and oblige them to represent the free democratic basic order. The fear of populism is evident in the words of Hanna Ahrendt (see Chapter 4.16). In Germany, no referendums are provided for in the Basic Law and they are limited to quorums at country level (see Chapter 6.3).

In Wikipedia, the term 'democracy theory' includes this statement: "John David Garcia expresses one of the many misunderstandings about democratic rule, also strengthened by media coverage: *"It is a cruel form of self-deception to believe that decisions reached by a large majority would automatically be ethical and correct".*

However, the model of democracy in Switzerland and empirical research[95] has shown that popular votes are rational. Rational decisions do not meet ethical norms, as the statement 'becoming innocent guilty' shows. Whether a decision was correct can only be assessed in retrospect. A decision by many people, however, is not subject to the parlamentary constraints. The parliamentary pressure, the party book or the influence of lobbyists determine the majority in parliament.

Monetary democracy is not a referendum. You can put fear of the minority at the back of monetary democracy. The dogma, as I call Walter Lippmann's position, that the people should be led by an elite, can be abolished in many areas.

8.13 Privatisations are good

What advantages do private companies offer? There are several criteria for success:

- Qualified, motivated employees in a supportive environment,

- ➢ The mission statement of the company must lead to the lasting existence of the company (e.g. 100 % quality, the customer is king, ...),
- ➢ Creativity in new product developments,
- ➢ Internal organisational adaptation to changed framework conditions (e.g. hierarchical principle against teamwork; use of new technologies such as the Internet ...).

How can you recognize the success of a company? In the 1960s, stock corporations published their balance sheets once a year. From the USA, the ¼ annual publications of company figures also swept to Germany. This only makes sense for investors, as they can guess the tendencies of the expected profit and the tenor of the share price.

Thus company investments (shares) became speculative papers. The profit maximisation principle of the investors moved into the foreground. Management was now obliged to pay attention to share prices.

The concept of privatisation thus took on two meanings:

- ➢ The private sector works efficiently, as medium-sized companies usually prove.
- ✓ The efficiency of a company can be seen in its profit and share price.

This blending of two conflicting views led to the conviction that state, sluggish institutions and public utilities should be placed in private hands. This led to the PPP Acceleration Act (and amendment of the Constitution Article 90 on 13.07.2017), which was drafted by the Federal Finance Minister Peer Steinbrück. Investors are exempt from property tax when they purchase land for the construction of schools or town halls and do not need to provide proof of their existing equity capital[96].

This opened the way for investors to give free play to their short-term profitability interests of listed companies or participations in companies.

Another reason for the extensive privatisations was the chronic underfunding of public budgets. The proceeds from the sale of social housing buildings were used to plug huge budget holes. In doing so, the politicians elude responsibility towards the population. The sales contracts, the contracts of the public private partnerships of Toll Collect etc. are mostly secret and the government is often abused as hostage of the investors[97].

In the wave of privatisation, the federal government has 'since the beginning of the Kohl era' separated itself from more than 900 participations at the direct and indirect level. In the meantime, it only has over 100 holdings or less than 100 holdings, because the list of privatisation objects ranges from theatres, museums, swimming pools, universities and clinics to municipal housing associations and water, sewage and electricity works[98]. Further specific examples can be read by Prof. Dr. Tim Engartner in his lectures and publications.

With most privatisations it is the consequence that they become more expensive for the citizens, than if they remained further in the public hand.

Monetary democracy refrains from profit maximisation and takes into account the time horizon across generations. Using examples such as the expansion of the Internet (Chapter 5.4), monetary democracy respects the primacy of the Basic Law to create equal living conditions everywhere (GG Art. 72, Para. 2). The financial nature of the project (installations) recommends buying shares in electricity grid operators or power stations by wind and sun. Thus, a part of the infrastructure necessary for the future is withdrawn from the market of profit interests. Communities and cities can also use monetary democracy to buy back public utilities (water and wastewater utilities, power grids, waste disposal, etc.).

8.14 The majority principle is the basis of democracy

If one speaks with politically interested fellow citizens, then the majority principle voting is represented at the end as holy sacrilege, as Ultima Ratio. Using Turkey as an example, however, leading German politicians reminded us that almost half of the population voted against Mr Erdogan's election. In the Brexit referendum the press was criticised for its 'stupid' propaganda in the mass newspapers Daily Sun and Daily Mai[99]l.

If I look at the world as it has evolved historically and the freedoms of the individual, I deviate from the majority principle.

History has taught us, both negatively and positively, that minorities change the world over long periods of time. Karl Marx and Friedrich Engels laid the foundation for the communist ideology that shaped a whole century. Adolf Hitler with his 'supporters' started the Second World War and the genocide of the Jews. The history of the Enlightenment produced great thinkers who laid the foundation for the French Revolution. The constitutions of Western countries are based on these epochal insights into human evolution.

If the above examples are all stained with blood, then the scientific-technical development is bloodlessly created by minorities. The resulting industrial revolution forced changes in the existing balance of power. Today mankind is facing a revolution again: genetic engineering, big data, industry 4.0, AI are the challenges. A minority with a lot of capital forces us to new forms of life. Politics has the task of setting the course for our future. Laws should pave the way for change and prevent excesses[100].

This leads directly to the majority decision, which is an important component of monetary democracy: the rejection of projects.

Any construction measure in Germany must be approved by the authorities and other bodies, such as the local council. In special constellations, the permits of neighbours must also be submitted. At any time citizens can take legal action against a building measure, e.g. because of protection of species. In the case of the Stuttgart 21 project, a referendum was held on whether the project should be stopped. The monetary democracy falls back on this kind of majority decision: the rejection of projects.

Monetary democracy promotes the commitment, inventiveness and enthusiasm of minorities who want to realize environmental and climate projects. The time of the nerve-racking search for investors is eliminated, as the documentation on the storage of the generated wind power in pressure vessels shows[101]. This is how projects are tackled that work across generations and must be regarded as unattractive by investors in a capitalist society.

The majority principle for one thing promotes inactivity; the majority principle against one thing prevents undesirable developments.

8.15 Climate policy only works with international agreements

Climate change affects the whole earth and humanity. The United Nations Charter defines the sovereignty of individual countries. The logical conclusion is international agreements. However, international agreements can be terminated at any time and lead to crisis situations. This can be seen in the exit of the USA from the target of the Paris Agreement or from the treaty with Iran, which is also only temporary.

In addition, the individual countries are limited in their ability to act by international, economic and financial dependencies. It goes without saying that the rulers are obliged to their own people, either because of democratic elections or to maintain their own power.

The fight against climate change today requires the possibility for affected and committed people to take concrete action. Their actions can be directed against countries, their ignorant governments or against big business. It is time not only to give these minorities a public space for debate, but also the opportunity to put their ideas into practice. To this end, they must be given a source of funding, which monetary democracy can do worldwide.

In opposition to international agreements, monetary climate policy is not endangered in terms of efficiency if individual countries are unable to meet their voluntary commitment to an offset amount or withdraw from an agreement. Commitment comes neither from capital nor from the governments of individual countries - it comes from engaged citizens.

8.16 Only the country has the taxpayer's money at its disposal

Public budgets are chronically underfunded. Between the responsible areas, community, district, county, confederatve government, there are always distribution battles. Power is also associated with these distribution struggles. With this power politicians can present their achievements to the public. The publication of the inauguration of a motorway section in the newspaper is advertising for itself. An appearance with a symbol of aerospace implies to the elector that the politician can set the course for the future.

Monetary democracy returns the responsibility for a part of the tax revenues to the people. On the one hand, this deprives politicians of power and, on the other, avoids conflicts of competence. This relief will make politics more efficient.

8.17 Responsibilities of city, district ... are immovable

In the case of the road network or public schools, different responsibilities have historically grown in Germany. I regard this as a practical example of the subsidiarity principle. The people on the spot know better what needs to be done.

As soon as money comes into the game, however, there is a scramble for scarce finances. With common financial obligations, the community can be well equipped, the circle is financially tight, or vice versa - and the needed maintenance cannot be carried out. See the example in chapter 5.1.

If I look at a tenancy of an apartment, the tenants are responsible for the cleaning and operation of the object. Smaller repairs may also have to be paid for by the tenants themselves. For larger renovations, the house owner is responsible. This contractual relationship can be transferred to the public structures. The road network, schools or even hospitals are for the general public, for the people. Irrespective of the ownership and ownership situation, the 'tenant' is responsible for ongoing maintenance, i.e. the community, the district, the county or the federal government. In the case of major redevelopments, I see the sovereign who uses the facility, i.e. the people, as having a duty. When planning a structural change, e.g. school buildings, the government always has the option of rejecting a concrete project.

Monetary democracy returns not only the financing but also the decision-making power to the people. 'Take back control', as described in Chapter 4.8.

8.18 Alternative: public or private

As in the case of public services (see Chapter 8.13), the question arises as to whether infrastructure measures should be financed by public funds, including loans, or by private investors. I also see PPPs as an instrument that offers those responsible the alternative of having the house/street assembled or, at higher cost, transferring it to private investors (on a temporary basis).

Personally I know the following rule: if I have only one possibility, I am in a forced situation. If I have an alternative, I can only choose between two possibilities, with the known positive and negative effects. If I look for a third possibility, then the freedom to make a decision begins.

If I transfer this to politics, it is in a much stronger position due to several possibilities. If it does not find a majority solution in the decision-making committees, it can transfer the infrastructure measure to monetary democracy as a project for coordination and financing.

Monetary democracy has nothing to do with 'people's property' or communism. The infrastructures in public hands can remain there through monetary democracy.

8.19 Co-financing is unavoidable

In the EU, co-financing refers to a subsidy in which the recipient is required to pay its own contribution. In 2011, the contribution rates for 6 countries (Greece, Ireland, Portugal, Romania, Latvia and Hungary)[102] were raised to 95% because of budgetary constraints.

The justification for mixed financing can be, for example, the different responsibilities between community, district and country (see example chapter 5.1). The psychological background, however, seems to me to be that in the case of a co-payment, the recipient's own interest is to be expected, i.e. less 'fraud' takes place. As explained in chapter 4.10, subsidies, since they are there, are simply spent and partly not thought about the purpose. This reminds me of budget thinking. If there are still funds available at the end of the year, new writing desks are bought - otherwise the budget would be cut in the following year.

Monetary democracy goes other ways. Transparency is required for full financial reporting, in particular the names of the persons responsible. Not the money decides, but the sense of a project. Especially financially weak communities have to save and postpone necessary investments. The votes of the participants automatically determine urgency, benefit and financing.

9. Bibliography

[1] QD302: „Altruismus Versus Egoismus“, Folge 3, ARDα (26.10.2015)

[2] QD104: „Afrika, Wege aus der Armutsfalle“ Sendung MAKRO, 3SAT (25.09.2015)

[3] QD300: „Altruismus versus Egoismus“ Folge 2, ARDα (26.10 2015)

QD301: „Altruismus versus Egoismus“ Folge 1, ARDα, (26.10.2015)

QD302: „Altruismus Versus Egoismus“, Folge 3, ARDα (26.10.2015)

[4] QD112: „Die größten Baustellen Deutschlands“, Phoenix (12.10.2015)

[5] QD338: Der Europacheck, 3SAT (14.09.2018)

[6] QD339: „Hat sich die Vorstellung vom „mündigen Bürger“ überlebt?“ Prof. Dr. Rainer Mausfeld, Elitendemokratie und Meinungsmanagement, Teleakademie, SWR (02.12.2018)

[7] QD315: „Netzwerk der Mächtigen - von Schattenbanken und Megainvestoren“, Planet wissen, Interviewpartner Hans-Jürgen Jacobs, Buch: Wem gehört die Welt, ARDα (29. 07 2018)

[8] QD316: „Vorgelegter Bundeshaushalt für 2019“ Morgenmagazin ARD/ZDF (11. 09 2018)

[9] QD012: „Anleger in Not“, Sendung Makro, 3SAT (17.04.2015)

[10] QD302: „Altruismus Versus Egoismus“, Folge 3, ARDα (26.10.2015)

[11] QD309: Francis Fukojama, Autor des Buches: Political order and political decay, Square Idee, ARTE (10. 05 2015)

[12] QD334: „Ungehorsam in der Demokratie“, Sendereihe Philosophie, Arte (27.10.2018)

[13] QD312: Morgenmagazin, (07.11.2018)

[14] QD315: „Netzwerk der Mächtigen - von Schattenbanken und Megainvestoren“, Planet wissen, Interviewpartner Hans-Jürgen Jacobs, Buch: Wem gehört die Welt, ARDα (29. 07 2018)

[15] QD319: „Ausgebeutet und mishandelt - Grossbritanniens neue Sklaven“, ZDF Info, ähnliche Dokumentationen gibt es auch für Deutschland. (2017)

[16] QD312: Morgenmagazin, (07.11.2018)

[17] „Glaube und Profit“, MAKRO, 3SAT (27.03.2015)

[18] QD330: „Ungleichland – wie aus Reichtum Macht wird“, Story im 1., ARD (08.05.2018)

[19] QD322: „Glaube und Profit“, MAKRO, 3SAT (27.03.2015)

[20] Zitat aus der Quelle QD315: „Netzwerk der Mächtigen - von Schattenbanken und Megainvestoren“, Planet wissen, Interviewpartner Hans-Jürgen Jacobs, Buch: Wem gehört die Welt, ARDα (29.07.2018)

[21] QD315: „Netzwerk der Mächtigen - von Schattenbanken und Megainvestoren“, Planet wissen, Interviewpartner Hans-Jürgen Jacobs, Buch: Wem gehört die Welt, ARDα (29.07.2018)

[22] QD315: „Netzwerk der Mächtigen - von Schattenbanken und Megainvestoren“, Planet wissen, Interviewpartner Hans-Jürgen Jacobs, Buch: Wem gehört die Welt, ARDα (29.07.2018)

[23] QD322: „Glaube und Profit“, MAKRO, 3SAT (27.03.2015)

[24] QD322: „Glaube und Profit“, MAKRO, 3SAT (27.03.2015)

[25] QD317: „Brücke wird 13 Jahre nicht gebaut“, Drehscheibe, ZDF (11.09.2018)

[26] QD327: „Kostenfalle Kanalisation“, Phoenix (26.05.2015)

[27] QD337: Kulturzeit, 3SAT (21.11.2018)

[28] QD337: Kulturzeit, 3SAT (21.11.2018)

[29] QD338: Der Europacheck, 3SAT (14.09.2018)

[30] QD339: „Hat sich die Vorstellung vom „mündigen Bürger“ überlebt?“ Prof. Dr. Rainer Mausfeld, Elitendemokratie und Meinungsmanagement, Teleakademie, SWR (02.12.2018)

[31] QD341: „Deutsche Justiz - wie gefährdet ist unser Recht?“ Tagesschau 24, ARD/ZDF (12.11 2018)

[32] QD338: Der Europacheck, 3SAT (14.09.2018)

[33] QD303: „Spielplatz“, Sendung Drehscheibe, ZDF (14.09.2018)

[34] QD350: „Der Milliardenwahnsinn“, Phönix (10.03.2015)

[35] QD338: Der Europacheck, 3SAT (14.09.2018)

[36] QD338: Der Europacheck, 3SAT (14.09.2018)

[37] QD311: „Sparen für die Rente“ MAX-Das Marktmagazin, Tagesschau 24 (26.10.2018)

[38] QD102: „Wird der Kakao knapp?“ Sendung mit Offenen Karten, ARTE (26.09.2015)

[39] QD353: „Unantastbar – Der Kampf um Menschenrechte“, ARTE (30.11.2018)

[40] QD337: Kulturzeit, 3SAT (21.11.2018)

[41] QD332: ‚Rechtsextremismus‘, Sendung Kulturzeit, 3SAT (31.08.2018)

[42] QD313: „Update für die Demokratie“, Phoenix (19.02.2018)

[43] QD340: „Staat im Ausverkauf – Privatisierung in Deutschland“, Teleakademie, Prof. Dr. Tim Engartner, 3SAT (02.12.2018)

[44] QD313: „Update für die Demokratie“, Phoenix (19.02.2018)

[45] QD313: „Update für die Demokratie“, Phoenix (19.02.2018)

[46] QD305: „Wahlen in der Demokratie“ Kulturzeit, 3SAT (21.09.2018)

[47] QD355 „Das Dieseldesaster“, ARD (07.01.2019)

[48] QD301: „Altruismus versus Egoismus“ Folge 1, ARDα, (26.10.2015)

[49] QD339: „Hat sich die Vorstellung vom „mündigen Bürger“ überlebt?“ Prof. Dr. Rainer Mausfeld, Elitendemokratie und Meinungsmanagement, Teleakademie, SWR (02.12.2018)

[50] QD340: „Staat im Ausverkauf – Privatisierung in Deutschland“, Teleakademie, Prof. Dr. Tim Engartner, 3SAT (02.12.2018)

[51] QD326: „Die Chinesen ersticken“, Sendung mit offenen Karten, ARTE (15.05.2015)

[52] QD347: „Die Welt des Xi Jinping“, Dokumentation Frankreich 2018, ARTE (18.12.2018)

[53] QD317: „Brücke wird 13 Jahre nicht gebaut“, Drehscheibe, ZDF (11.09.2018)

[54] QD318: „Stadtentwicklung und Vermögensverwaltung“, Kulturzeit, ARTE (14.11.2018)

[55] QD349: „Spitzengespräche, Kreise, Kommunen und Land beraten Kommunalpakt“, Daten der Woche vom Sonntag, 23.12.2018, Tagesschau 24 (23.12.2018)

[56] QD323: „Windiges Geld“, Tagesschau24 (03.04.2015)

[57] QD004: „Pakt mit dem Panda“, WDR/SRW, 1Extra (27.06.2011)

[58] QD352: Sendung Plus Minus, ARD (12.11.2015)

[59] QD353: „Unantastbar – Der Kampf der Menschenrechte“, ARTE (30.11.218)

[60] QD354 „Prima Klima?“ MAKRO, 3SAT (30.11.2018)

[61] QD356: „Ein Erfinder macht Druck für die Energiewende, Phoenix (09.08.2018)

[62] QD340: „Staat im Ausverkauf – Privatisierung in Deutschland“, Teleakademie, Prof. Dr. Tim Engartner, 3SAT (02.12.2018)

[63] QD329: „Demokratie in Not“, Planet Wissen, SWR (03.04.2018)

[64] QD329: „Demokratie in Not“, Planet Wissen, SWR (03.04.2018)

[65] QD357:https://rp.baden-wuerttemberg.de/rpk/Abt4/Ref44/Seiten/B293_Ortsumgehung_Joehlingen.aspx

[66] QD307: „Neuer Weltklimareport“ Arte Journal (08.10.2018)

[67] QD323: „Windiges Geld“, Tagesschau24 (03.04.2015)

[68] QD304: „CO_2-Belastung durch Flugverkehr“ Sendung Panorama, ARD (20.09.2018)

[69] QD351: Face to Face, „Wie sähe es aus, denn Autoabgase sichtbar wären?“, Ausgabe 11-2012/2013 Schülerzeitung der Beruflichen Schulen Bretten

[70] QD304: „CO_2-Belastung durch Flugverkehr“ Sendung Panorama, ARD (20.09.2018)

[71] QD003: „Abgefackelt“ Produktion NDR, ARTE (28.06.2011)

[72] QD003: „Abgefackelt“ Produktion NDR, ARTE (28.06.2011)

[73] QI007: Finanzierung von „Erneuerbare-Energien-Projekten in Lateinamerika und der Karibik“, BMWi-Fachveranstaltung, http://www.export-erneuerbare.de/EEE/Redaktion/DE/Veranstaltungen/2015/Infoveranstaltungen/fv-finanzierung-lateinamerika.html

[74] QI020: Desertec Foundation, http://www.desertec.org/de/

[75] QI022: „Baden in Natronlauge“ und Greenpeace Magazin 1.98 „Rostfraß an Giftgasmunition“

[76] QI022: „Baden in Natronlauge“ und Greenpeace Magazin 1.98 „Rostfraß an Giftgasmunition“

[77] QD025: "Könnes kämpft - Fassadendämmung - Das Märchen vom Energiesparen" WDR, nicht mehr in der Mediathek abrufbar (11/2014)

[78] QI021: „Wärmedämmung: Teuer, ungesund und leicht entflammbar“ http://www.br.de/nachrichten/waermedaemmung-sanierung-100.html

[79] QD301: „Altruismus versus Egoismus“ Folge 2, ARDα, (26.10.2015)

[80] QD301: „Altruismus versus Egoismus“ Folge 1, ARDα, (26.10.2015)

[81] QD301: „Altruismus versus Egoismus“ Folge 1, ARDα, (26.10.2015)

[82] QD301: „Altruismus versus Egoismus“ Folge 1, ARDα, (26.10.2015)

[83] Quelle QD300 – QD302, see number 3

[84] QD300: „Altruismus versus Egoismus“ Folge 2, ARDα (26.10.2015)

[85] QD358: Exakt – so leben wir! Geben oder Nehmen?, Tagesschau24 (20.12.2018)

[86] QD355: Die Story: Die geheimen Machenschaften der Ölindustrie „Wie Energiekonzerne den Klimawandel vertuschen“ (WDR 2017) Tagesschau24 (06.01.2019)

[87] QD303: „Spielplatz“, Sendung Drehscheibe, ZDF (14.09 2018)

[88] QD300: „Altruismus versus Egoismus“ Folge 2, ARDα (26.10.2015)

[89] QD301: „Altruismus versus Egoismus“ Folge 1,ARDα, (26.10.2015)

[90] QD301: „Altruismus versus Egoismus“ Folge 1,ARDα, (26.10.2015)

[91] QD300: „Altruismus versus Egoismus“ Folge 2, ARDα (26.10.2015)

[92] QD315: „ Netzwerk der Mächtigen – von Schattenbanken und Megainvestoren“, Planet wissen, Interviewpartner Hans-Jürgen Jacobs, Buch: Wem gehört die Welt, ARDα <829.07.2018)

[93] QD308: „Klimawandel“, Kulturzeit, 3SAT (26.03.2015)

[94] QD339: „Hat sich die Vorstellung vom „mündigen Bürger“ überlebt?“ Prof. Dr. Rainer Mausfeld, Elitendemokratie und Meinungsmanagement, Teleakademie, SWR (02.12.2018)

[95] QD339: „Hat sich die Vorstellung vom „mündigen Bürger“ überlebt?“ Prof. Dr. Rainer Mausfeld, Elitendemokratie und Meinungsmanagement, Teleakademie, SWR (02.12.2018)

[96] QD340: „Staat im Ausverkauf – Privatisierung in Deutschland“, Teleakademie, Prof. Dr. Tim Engartner, 3SAT (02.12.2018)

[97] QD340: „Staat im Ausverkauf – Privatisierung in Deutschland“, Teleakademie, Prof. Dr. Tim Engartner, 3SAT (02.12.2018)

[98] QD340: „Staat im Ausverkauf – Privatisierung in Deutschland“, Teleakademie, Prof. Dr. Tim Engartner, 3SAT (02.12.2018)

[99] QD338: Der Europacheck, 3SAT (14.09.2018)

[100] QD356: „Ein Erfinder macht Druck für die Energiewende, Phoenix (09.08.2018)

[101] QD356: „Ein Erfinder macht Druck für die Energiewende, Phoenix (09.08.2018)

[102] QD359: https://ec.europa.eu/social/main.jsp?langId=de&catId=325&newsId=1061&furtherNews=yes